Playing with Media

simple ideas for powerful sharing

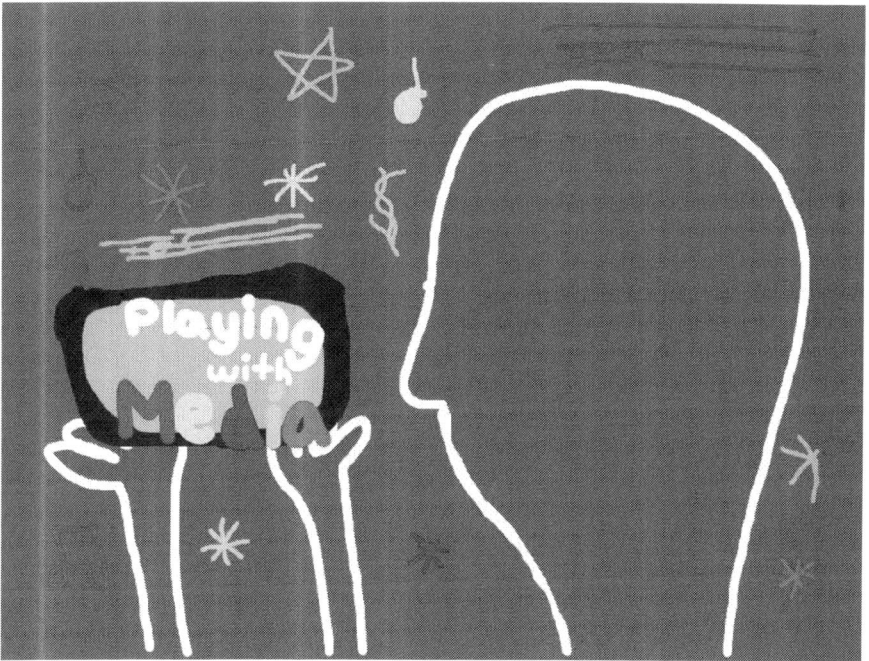

by Wesley A. Fryer
Illustrations by Rachel C. Fryer

---

paperback Version 1.0 (August 2011)
www.playingwithmedia.com

"Uses of technology which require fewer clicks can be naturally adopted by a larger percentage of educators than those which are more complex and cumbersome. **Digital simplicity matters**."

- *Wesley Fryer*

Legal Stuff and Links

This is the **paperback** version of this eBook. eBook versions are available and linked from http://playingwithmedia.com/pages/about. Underlined words and phrases are hyperlinked in eBook versions. Full URLs (web addresses) are included in footnote citations.

Illustrations by Rachel Fryer. Rachel (age 7) created digital art for this book using the Brushes application and a Rocketfish stylus on an iPad. Visit Rachel's web show, "The Zebra Print," on www.thezebraprint.com.

Access related resources for and updates to this book on www.playingwithmedia.com. Provide feedback including suggestions, book reviews, and your own media project links to share using contact forms on www.playingwithmedia.com/pages/feedback. When tweeting about this book and sharing your inspired media creations, please use the Twitter hashtag #playingwithmedia. When posting related media please use the tag "playingwithmedia" without quotation marks.

Access Wesley Fryer's "digital footprint" via his Google profile on profiles.google.com/wesfryer. Follow him on Twitter @wfryer. Read and subscribe to his blog, "Moving at the Speed of Creativity," on www.speedofcreativity.org. Contact details for Wesley are available on www.wesfryer.com/contact.

Praise for Playing with Media

@tedrosececi
Alison Anderson

@wfryer **reading** #playingwithmedia I think Al Gore's ebook is cool but your book is EXACTLY what an ebook should be! Great PD to end summer!

7 Aug via Twitter for iPad

"There are plenty of books out there that are tapping into the tools of the 21st Century, and Fryer's ebook should join the mix of some of the more useful and interesting out there right now. His engaging writing style, inclusion of very useful resources and tutorials, sharing of authentic examples and explanations of the pedagogy behind the technology make for an enjoyable and productive read. I highly recommend Playing with Media: Simple Tools for Powerful Sharing for any Kindle, Nook, iPad or whatever your device might be."

- Kevin Hodgson, Sixth grade teacher in Southampton, Massachusetts, and the technology liaison with the Western Massachusetts Writing Project.

I like how Wes has examples to illustrate his ideas, which leads the reader, inter-actor, teammate, actor, playmate, viewer, listener, and creator to engage with this ebook. Wes gives all of us permission to play in the sandbox. He gives us strategies to try as we move along in the book. He gives us enough history so we are grounded and understand that "We learn deeper when we actively DO rather than passively watch."

- Cheryl Oakes, High School Resource Teacher, Wells, Maine

"I am a homeschool mom to three little girls and I recently began searching for ways to use technology in our classroom. I'm not talking about internet searches for curriculum reviews or "educational" games to occupy the kids while I get a grasp on my sanity; I'm talking about learning to create digital "artifacts" and portfolios and learning to connect with other educators beyond my current homeschool forum. I'm NOT tech savvy and I was struggling to find someone to explain the wild, wooly world of creating blogs, wikis, audio and video stories, etc.

I was following Mr. Fryer on Twitter when I heard about his book. I downloaded the sample and was hooked after reading just the table of contents (which is linked). This was exactly what I needed. I went on to read the acknowledgements and was introduced to several fascinating people via Twitter. I downloaded the entire book and stayed up till 3 am reading. Mr. Fryer uses many, many links on nearly every page. He links to definitions to explain new terminology to newbies, like me. He links to examples of programs, movies, apps, and more. Everything was very well explained.

If you don't own a Kindle, don't despair! I read through it the first time on my Kindle then the next day I downloaded the Kindle app to my computer. I've been re-reading the book on my laptop in order to access the audio and video links as well as the websites."

- Rachel Donnell, Homeschooling parent in Maryland

"I work with teachers who use technology to support their classroom instruction. Wes Fryer's new e-book, Playing with Media, has arrived just in time for school to start. Remember "make and take" workshops? This is it for the digital classroom. It is exactly the kind of book that should accompany any teacher workshop or training because it supports great teaching. It will be an invaluable resource all year long. It is relevant to any classroom in both pedagogy and instruction. The book is presented in a succinct, understandable manner. There are tools, explained with clear directions and graphics; big ideas, and follow up reading. Taken together, these will have a profound impact on any classroom. Everything is clickable. And the fact that's it's an ebook means that Wes will keep it up to date.

The more I read through and listened, the more excited I got. Not only did I learn many little tips and tricks, the reminder that we must keep creativity in our curriculum is ever present. I also enjoyed how Wes used his own children as models to showcase student work. He is passionate about sharing and celebrating what students can do on the web. In each category multiple tools are shown, modeling creation choice for student projects.

I chose to download and read the versions on my iPad and Kindle. The Kindle experience was less hands on but still easy to read. There is a companion website to go with the book. There is so much in this book that I will be using the resources time and time again. I really appreciated how this book is organized and would highly recommend it. I would love to see other classroom books modeled on this kind of ebook. I am going to think about it as a text book for a professional development course that I teach to education graduate students. #playingwithmedia"

- Alice Barr, High School Technology Integration Specialist, Yarmouth, Maine

"This book, in my opinion, should be required reading for principals, academic coordinators and most teachers across the United States who continue to struggle with or just flat out ignore 21st century learning tools and strategies. Fryer's rich infusion of graphics, links, video and creativeness makes this book an inspiring and powerful experience for the reader/listener/viewer. It's virtually everything you'd expect from a "new" book. "Playing With Media..." virtually lifts the bookshelf!.

- H. Songhai, Technology Coordinator, HOPE Charter School, Philadelphia, Pennsylvania

Table of Contents

Acknowledgements

This book is dedicated to my children: Alexander, Sarah and Rachel, who inspire me to play with media and continually strive to become a better teacher.

I want to express special thanks to my wife, Shelly, as well as my children, who regularly demonstrate amazing patience with their husband and father who frequently enlists their assistance with media projects. Many of our experiences learning with media are archived on our family learning blog, "Learning Signs," accessible on learningsigns.speedofcreativity.org.

Thanks to my parents, Tom and Angie, who first introduced me to the importance, art and skills of communication. Thanks also to my mother for helping me edit and proof this book. Thanks to Jim Bogart, who first introduced me to the wonders of darkroom photography in the 7th grade and later taught me how to "play with images" using slide projectors and a dissolve unit for our high school AFS student assembly presentations in 1984-85 in Manhattan, Kansas. Thanks to my parents and in-laws, Carl and Clara Ward, whose support has opened professional doors for me which otherwise would have remained closed.

Thanks to the inventors, engineers, scientists and geeks who built the infrastructure of the technium which makes the publication of this book possible.[1]

Thanks to my friends and professional collaborators who have helped shape my mind and challenge me to imagine new possibilities each day. Specifically, thanks to Miguel Guhlin whose acts of selfless, digital sharing continue to inspire me to be an educational change agent. Thanks to David Warlick, whose ideas encouraged me to

---

[1] Kelly, K. (2007, February 23). Major Stages of the Technium. The Technium. Retrieved June 4, 2011, from http://www.kk.org/thetechnium/archives/2007/02/major_stages_of.php

embrace a grander vision of education and learning than most people could see in my 4th grade classroom. Thanks to Bob Sprankle, whose blogging, podcasting, and media creation activities with students first challenged me to become a digital storyteller and a storychaser. Thanks to David Jakes, who opened my eyes to the possibilities of digital storytelling for empowering students to discover and share their voices. If you don't already "follow" these amazing minds on Twitter, you need to. My debt to them and MANY others is greater than I can ever repay.

Many thanks to Dana Owens-Delong, Dawn Danker, and Don Wilson whose work and support has been pivotal in the the development of my career as a digital learning consultant as well as the formation of Story Chasers Inc. Thanks also to Kevin Honeycutt, Dean Mantz, and Cyndi Danner-Kuhn whose friendship and continual encouragement inspires me.

Thanks to Charlene Chausis (presentation links) and Carolyn Foote (audio podcast and presentation links) for helping educate me about eBooks, the differences in eBook formats, and the publication possibilities eBooks offer today.

I owe a tremendous learning debt to my fellow organizers of the free, K-12 Online Conference (www.k12onlineconference.org) and the amazing presenters who have shared inspiring ideas for using educational technology in creative ways there since 2006. If you are not "plugged in" to the K-12 Online Conference yet, I'll offer this caution: It very well might change your life. Connecting to other creative educators not only for a conference event but on an ongoing basis continues to be the most powerful engine of my professional learning as an educator.

Last of all, thanks to YOU for reading and considering these thoughts. I am honored to have this opportunity to swap some ideas with you. I look forward to reading, hearing and watching your feedback. :-)

1- Why?

"Playing with Media" by Rachel Fryer [2]

(If you're already confident about the importance of "playing with media," you can skip ahead to the next chapter on "Digital Text.")

We live in a wonderful age for learning.

As I write these words, I marvel at the amazing opportunities available for not only accessing the ideas of others but also sharing our own. When Martin Luther penned the 95 Theses in 1517 I doubt he dreamed people on our planet would live in an

---

[2] Fryer, R. (2011, June 21). Playing With Media (book cover by Rachel Fryer). Flickr - Photo Sharing. Retrieved July 22, 2011, from http://www.flickr.com/photos/wfryer/5856708953/in/set-72157626886284140

environment like ours today, where we are increasingly challenged by our need to filter large quantities of information rather than simply gain access to them.[3]   Literacy has changed dramatically and continues to change. As learners and leaders, our skills need to change as well.

This book is written primarily for educators, but I welcome anyone as a reader who is interested in learning how to more flexibly, creatively, and effectively communicate with media in our digital age. **My primary goal is to inspire and empower you**, as a creative person, to "play with media" in a variety of formats to expand your personal senses of digital literacy and digital agency as a multimedia communicator.

I have subtitled this book, "simple ideas for powerful sharing," because playing and learning are best done with others. As you read, watch, listen and link to ideas connected to this book, I invite you to create, play, and share. The title, "Playing with Media" may strike some as frivolous, but let me assure you this is serious work. Douglas Thomas and John Seely Brown remind us in their recent book, "A New Culture of Learning," as children we progressively make sense of our confusing world through play.[4]   This process of making meaning through play continues into adulthood, although as adults we often refrain from overt, visible play in our workplaces. The dynamic media landscape in which we live can be confusing, however, and we need to PLAY with different forms of media to understand their capabilities as well as develop our own skills of expression using them.

---

[3] The Ninety-Five Theses - Wikipedia, the free encyclopedia. (n.d.). Wikipedia, the free encyclopedia. Retrieved June 2, 2011, from http://en.wikipedia.org/wiki/The_Ninety-Five_Theses

[4] Thomas, D., & Brown, J. S. (2011). A new culture of learning: cultivating the imagination for a world of constant change. Lexington, KY: s.n.]. http://www.newcultureoflearning.com/

As educators, I believe "playing with media" is a necessary and pre-requisite step towards effectively integrating the use of media effectively within classroom instruction. I hope each educator reading these words will not only take time to play with media, but also apply the knowledge and skills gained from these experiences within student lessons designed for 21st century learners.

Merriam-Webster offers nine definitions of the word, "book."[5] None of these, however, precisely summarize this specific writing project which has electronic/digital as well as paper-based/analog forms. Using the ebook form of this work, readers can not only hyperlink to referenced resources but also watch videos including screencasts of suggested communication techniques.[6] All referenced screencasts are listed (with direct website links / URLs) in a concluding chapter. The process of consuming and processing this book in its digital form is more than simply "reading." Like communication more broadly today, reading and learning are processes which involve multiple forms of media. For reasons I'm about to highlight, we all need to spend more time playing with media.

I used the free iPad application Popplet Lite (popplet.com) to brainstorm many of the reasons WHY we need to play with media. A screenshot of one of those those mind maps is shown below. It served as a visual and textual outline of the ideas which eventually coalesced to become this book.

---

[5] Book - Definition and More from the Free Merriam-Webster Dictionary. (n.d.). Dictionary and Thesaurus - Merriam-Webster Online. Retrieved June 2, 2011, from http://www.merriam-webster.com/dictionary/book

[6] Screencast - Wikipedia, the free encyclopedia. (n.d.). Wikipedia, the free encyclopedia. Retrieved June 2, 2011, from http://en.wikipedia.org/wiki/Screencast

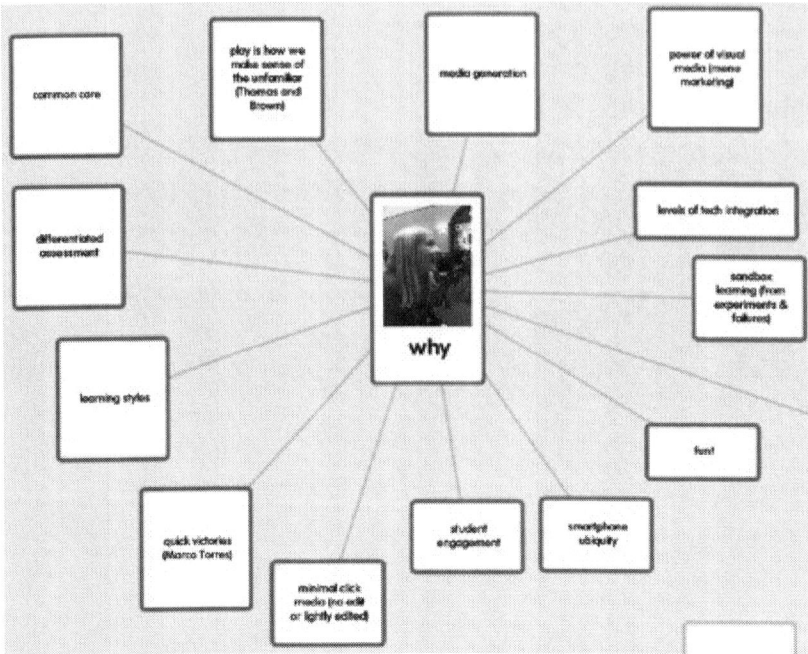

Why Play With Media by Wesley Fryer [7]

A Media Generation

Author Marc Prensky gained considerable notoriety in educational technology circles following publication of his 2001 article, "Digital Natives, Digital Immigrants."[8] In the article and numerous presentations around the United States at educational

---

[7] Fryer, W. (2011, June 4). Why Play with Media?. Flickr - Photo Sharing. Retrieved July 24, 2011, from http://www.flickr.com/photos/wfryer/5798490416/in/set-72157626886284140

[8] Prensky, M. (2001, October). Digital Natives, Digital Immigrants. On the Horizon, Vol. 9, No. 5.
from http://www.marcprensky.com/writing/prensky%20-%20digital%20natives,%20digital%20immigrants%20-%20part1.pdf

technology conferences, Prensky preached a simple message regarding youth and media: The younger generation "gets it," the older folks don't. This message has a psychological appeal for many adults both apprehensive and ignorant about many of the communication possibilities latent within our digital media landscape. Unfortunately, it can be used as an excuse by adults to abstain from participation in technology-powered conversations with social media and other tools. Teachers who say, "I don't do technology, I'm a digital immigrant," personify this regrettable attitude.

We are living in dynamic times, and the ascendent generations ARE much more comfortable consuming as well as creating media than their predecessors. The "Digital Generation" video project by EduTopia highlighted many of the ways today's students are different because of their access and uses of media both at home and school. The project's authors describe our students this way:

> Today's kids are born digital -- born into a
> media-rich, networked world of infinite
> possibilities. But their digital lifestyle is about
> more than just cool gadgets; it's about
> engagement, self-directed learning, creativity,
> and empowerment. The Digital Generation
> Project tells their stories so that educators and
> parents can understand how kids learn,
> communicate, and socialize in very different
> ways than any previous generation.[9]

Unlike Prensky's article, which encouraged some teachers to define themselves as "digital immigrants" who can opt out of technologically-powered learning, EduTopia's Digital Generation project presents a compelling case for the reasons educators today

---

[9] The Digital Generation Project. (n.d.). EduTopia: K-12 Education & Learning Innovations with Proven Strategies that Work. Retrieved June 4, 2011, from http://www.edutopia.org/digital-generation

MUST embrace uses of media for learning. Age and generational differences do not have to define us entirely as learners. Older dogs CAN learn new tricks.

In addition to avoiding the temptation to reclusively hide under the label, "digital immigrant," educators today should also avoid the pitfall of assuming "digital natives" are digitally literate. Comfort using Facebook and watching YouTube videos does not equate to capacities to think critically or create persuasive digital content online. We should not mistake digital use for digital understanding or communications fluency. In "Digital refugees and bridges," my October 2006 post for Google's Education blog, The Infinite Thinking Machine, I highlighted our need as educators to serve as "digital bridges" rather than digital immigrants or digital refugees in our schools, homes and communities.[10]

---

[10] Fryer, W. (2006, October 20). Digital refugees and bridges. The Infinite Thinking Machine. Retrieved June 4, 2011, from http://www.infinitethinkingmachine.org/2006_10_15_archive.html

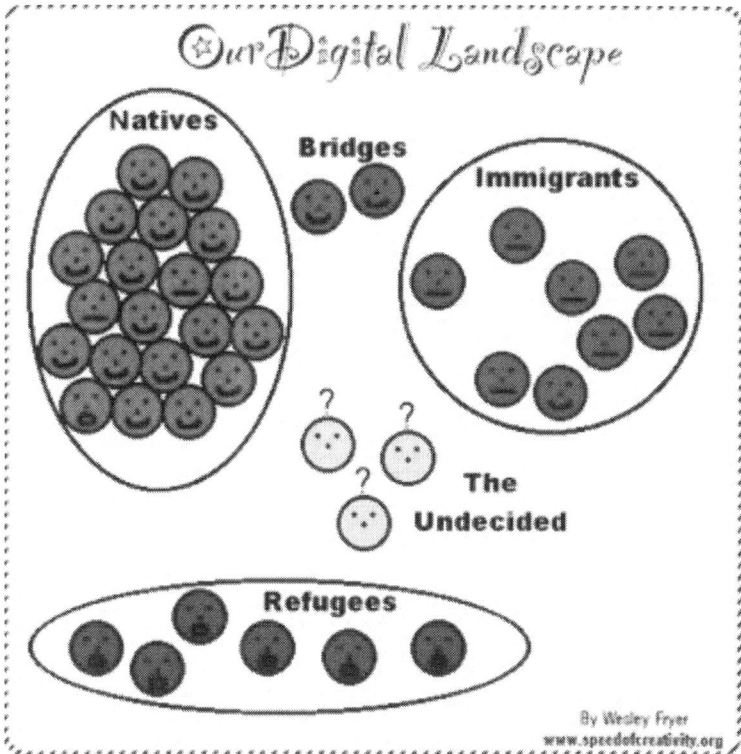

Our Digital Landscape by Wesley Fryer [11]

As the crude graphic I created in ClarisWorks / AppleWorks Draw highlighted, the "digital bridges" today in our digital landscape are outnumbered by natives, immigrants, refugees, and "the undecided." Educators in our schools who perceive we have a choice about using media effectively to help our students learn do so at their own peril and at a high potential cost. As educators, our continued relevance to and effectiveness with members of the ascendent media generation relies to a large extent on our abilities to effectively leverage the power of media to support learning. **The mere use of technology does not constitute or guarantee good teaching.**

---

[11] AppleWorks. (n.d.). Wikipedia, the free encyclopedia. Retrieved June 4, 2011, from http://en.wikipedia.org/wiki/AppleWorks

Good teachers always strive to find effective ways to reach, inspire, and engage students in the learning process, however, and media technologies have potent capacities to enhance learning. Outstanding teachers in the twenty-first century, like their predecessors, will be defined not only by their content knowledge but also by the effective ways they are able to inspire, relate to, and motivate students to stretch beyond their acknowledged limits. Technology should and will play an integral role in these processes of growth for students. To utilize media effectively with younger generations of students, we need to "play with media" as educators to better understand its capabilities as well as effective uses.

Images are Powerful

Just as marketers utilize images effectively to attract and maintain our attention on restaurant menus, roadside billboards, television and Internet webpages, as educators we need to leverage the power of visual literacy in our classroom lessons and assignments. It is impossible to go through the check-out area of a Walmart store without experiencing image-based marketing, as shown in the photo below.

Checkout stand media marketing [12]

Lynell Burmark, author of the book "Visual Literacy," cites research indicating the human eye processes images much faster than text, and thousands of times faster than messages we hear and process through our ears.[13] When we visually process text as readers of the English language, our eyes naturally start at the top of the page and move from left to right, top to bottom. In contrast, when viewing a photograph, no one "tells your eye" where to begin processing different areas of the image. Visual media can

---

[12] Fryer, W. (2009, January 11). Magazines in the checkout stand at Wal Mart. Flickr - Photo Sharing. Retrieved June 4, 2011, from http://www.flickr.com/photos/wfryer/3231168533/

[13] Burmark, L. (2002). Visual literacy: learn to see, see to learn. Alexandria, Va.: Association for Supervision and Curriculum Development.

communicate multiple messages with viewers which can build background knowledge, make explicit as well as implied connections, and connect new ideas to existing knowledge, or "schema." Just as it's impossible to read the menu at a restaurant like Chili's without processing images alongside text, learning experiences in our classrooms for students should be filled with visual media created and shared by students as well as teachers.

Visual menu marketing at Chili's [14]

---

[14] Fryer, W. (2009, January 11). Magazines in the checkout stand at Wal Mart. Flickr - Photo Sharing. Retrieved June 4, 2011, from http://www.flickr.com/photos/wfryer/3231168533/

Portfolio & Differentiated Assessment

For a variety of political as well as psychological factors, politicians in the United States in the past decade have been enamored with high stakes testing in our K-12 schools.[15] The destructive effects of that focus on our students, their workforce skills, their curriculum, their creativity, and the teachers who instruct them are not the focus of this book.[16] The fact that standardized assessments, typically implemented through the use of bubble sheets for student answers, provide an incomplete picture of student skills as well as dispositions IS relevant to the topics addressed here, however.

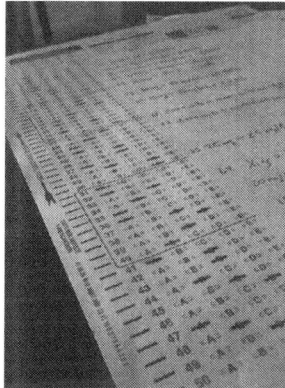

The Bubblesheet [17]

---

[15] High-stakes testing. (n.d.). Wikipedia, the free encyclopedia. Retrieved June 5, 2011, from http://en.wikipedia.org/wiki/High-stakes_testing

[16] Graves, D. H. (2002). Testing Is Not Teaching: What Should Count in Education. Portsmouth, NH: Heinemann.

[17] Miller, J. D. (n.d.). Stress. Flickr - Photo Sharing. Retrieved June 21, 2011, from http://www.flickr.com/photos/justin_d_miller/5139225141. Licensed under a Creative Commons Attribution-Only license.

We need to embrace differentiated forms of student assessment to better understand and reflect student knowledge and skills. When students are empowered to express their ideas with audio, images, video and digital text, other people can often access a larger window into the knowledge and skills of those students. As educators and parents, this can be valuable and insightful.

Good assessments begin with good questions. As you play with different types of media, try to answer as well as ask good questions which challenge you (and your students) to engage in higher order thinking. Anderson and Krathwohl's 2001 revision to Bloom's Taxonomy changed the words of each level in the framework into VERBS and placed CREATE at the top of the pyramid.

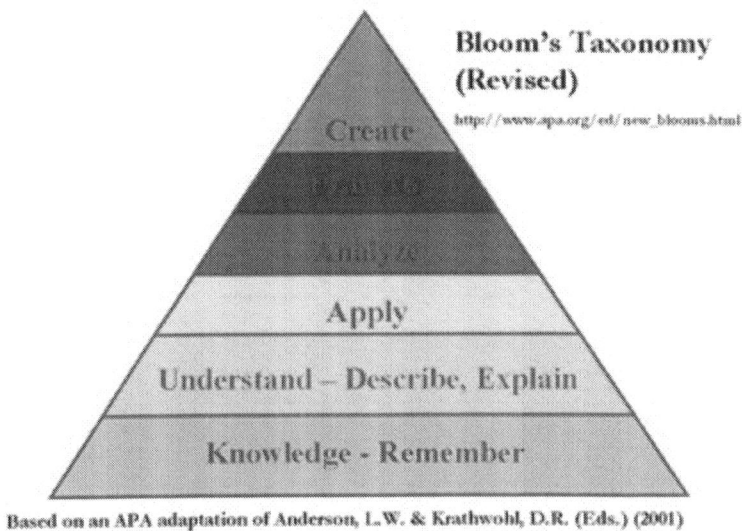

Bloom's Taxonomy (Revised)
http://www.apa.org/ed/new_blooms.html

Create

Analyze

Apply

Understand – Describe, Explain

Knowledge - Remember

Based on an APA adaptation of Anderson, L.W. & Krathwohl, D.R. (Eds.) (2001)

Bloom's 2001 Revised Taxonomy [18]

---

[18] The Revised Bloom's Taxonomy. (n.d.). Flickr - Photo Sharing. Retrieved June 21, 2011, from http://www.flickr.com/photos/wfryer/361710524/

When we CREATE as we are playing with
only showcase the lower-level knowledge an
learning which is reflected most easily in standard
but also the results of higher order thinking   ...entiated
assessment means providing diverse, media-rich options for students
to demonstrate their learning and understanding of studied topics.
Differentiated assessments can also provide opportunities for students
to develop and demonstrate their mastery of "digital literacies" and
twenty-first century literacy skills. Many of these skills are included
in the ISTE-NETS (International Society for Technology in
Education National Educational Technology Standards) for
Students.[19]

As we create with media to demonstrate our knowledge and
skills, we can potentially create "digital knowledge artifacts." These
digital files can be archived online as well as locally, and become part
of a growing digital portfolio of work. Helen Barrett
(electronicportfolios.com) and Philip Abrami define electronic
portfolios as:

> digital containers capable of storing visual and
> auditory content; software for which may also
> be designed to support a variety of
> pedagogical processes and assessment
> purposes.[20]

---

[19] International Society for Technology in Education. (n.d.). NETS
for Students . ISTE | NETS Standards. Retrieved June 21, 2011,
from http://www.iste.org/standards/nets-for-students.aspx

[20] Abrami, P. C., & Barrett, H. (2005). Directions for Research and
Development on Electronic Portfolios. Canadian Journal of
Learning and Technology / La revue canadienne de l'apprentissage
et de la technologie, 31(3). Retrieved June 21, 2011, from http://
www.cjlt.ca/index.php/cjlt/article/view/92/86

...le digital or electronic portfolios have been used most ...uently in pre-service teacher education programs in the United States to date, these "digital containers" can and should be used by K-12 students and teachers throughout their educational careers. In his presentation, "What Did You Do in School Yesterday, Today, and Three Years Ago" for the K-12 Online Conference, Philadelphia educator H. Songhai challenged listeners to consider the permanency of analog "evidences" of learning. In contrast, digital artifacts combined into a hyperlinked, digital portfolio can usefully persist in our information landscape for a much longer time. The need to help students craft digital portfolios which authentically and effectively represent their knowledge, skills, and accomplishments as learners is an important reason we all need more time "playing with media."

For additional resources and lesson ideas related to Bloom's Taxonomy and technologies, refer to Andrew Churches' "Bloom's Digital Taxonomy" on his Educational Origami website.[21]

Cell Phones Everywhere

Everyone does not have a cell phone, but a growing number of people in the developed and developing world (including students in our classrooms) do. According to the New Media Consortium's 2010 Horizon Report: K12 Edition:

> For many people all over the world, but
> especially in developing countries, where
> cellular access to the Internet is outpacing
> more traditional networks, mobiles are
> increasingly the gateway not only for common

---

[21] Churches, A. (n.d.). Bloom's Digital Taxonomy. Educational Origami. Retrieved June 21, 2011, from http://edorigami.wikispaces.com/Bloom's+Digital+Taxonomy

tools and communications, but also for information of all kinds, training materials, income-generating work, and more. An ever more common pattern is for people in all parts of the world to look to mobile computing platforms as their device of choice, as they are often far cheaper than desktop or laptop computers. For this group, mobile computing devices are more affordable, more accessible, and easier to use than desktop computers, and provide more than enough functionality to serve as their primary computing device... The portability of mobile devices and their ability to connect to the Internet almost anywhere makes them ideal as a store of reference materials and learning experiences, as well as general-use tools for field work, where they can be used to record observations via voice, text, or multimedia, and access reference sources in real time.[22]

While policies governing the use of cell phones by students in many United States schools remain restrictive, an enlightened minority of educational leaders is recognizing the power and potential of mobile devices to be used constructively in the learning process. Cell phones can not only serve as telecommunication devices for synchronous voice conversations, but also as mobile computing platforms capable of publishing as well as accessing a variety of rich media. Learners need access to powerful tools to create and share media, and mobile devices are increasingly the "digital tools of choice" for those playing with media. Educators and educational

---

[22] Johnson, L., Smith, R., Levine, A., & Haywood, K. (n.d.). Two to Three Years: Mobiles. The 2010 Horizon Report: K-12 Edition. Retrieved June 21, 2011, from http://wp.nmc.org/horizon-k12-2010/chapters/mobiles/#7

institutions should embrace the media consumption and production capabilities of cell phones, including "smartphones" capable of running a variety of applications in addition to accessing Internet websites. These tools not only support greater access to published media, they also can empower learners to create and share their own digital artifacts as they master new knowledge and skills.

Creativity

As Clay Shirky observed in his TED Talk, "How cognitive surplus will change the world," media abundance works according to clear rules. As creative human beings, we generally need to create a LOT in order to make high QUALITY work. In Shirky's words, we only "get" powerful, creative examples of collaborative media sharing like Ushahidi when people create a lot of lolcats.[23] We need to play with media frequently because when we play long enough, we create some remarkable things.

This idea was expressed in a story shared by David Bayles in his book, Art & Fear: Observations On the Perils (and Rewards) of Artmaking. Bayles tells a story of two groups of students in a ceramics class. One was graded based on the quantity of ceramics created in the term, and the other based on a single, finished project.

> Well, came grading time and a curious fact
> emerged: the works of highest quality were all
> produced by the group being graded for
> quantity. It seems that while the "quantity"
> group was busily churning out piles of work
> "and learning from their mistakes" the

---

[23] Shirky, C. (2010). How cognitive surplus will change the world | Video on TED.com. TED: Ideas worth spreading. Retrieved June 21, 2011, from http://www.ted.com/talks/ clay_shirky_how_cognitive_surplus_will_change_the_world.html

"quality" group had sat theorizing about perfection, and in the end had little more to show for their efforts than grandiose theories and a pile of dead clay.[24]

Creativity is important. Not only does creativity produce the innovations and technologies which make our lives easier and offer abundant choices in our modern world, it also produces artistic expressions which make our communities richer places to live.

CREATE is the root word of "creativity." As a teacher, if your students aren't MAKING STUFF they can't be creative. Without creation, there is no creativity. If the "final products" your students produce for an assignment in class all look the same, they haven't been given an authentic chance to be creative. Creativity can be messy. Creativity results in diverse outcomes. Participating in creative activities can help students get in touch with INTRINSIC reasons for doing something, rather than the "normal" EXTRINSIC reasons which are most often emphasized in school. (Grades, avoiding punishments, earning awards, etc.)

On a theological level, I believe as human beings we were created TO CREATE. Young children model this idea naturally. Although the draw of "the screen" (be it cinema, television, videogames, cell phones, mobile game systems, etc.) is powerful on young minds, we still see kids spontaneously participating in all kinds of artistic activities when given the opportunity, the time, and the tools. This innate desire to create, to make, to experiment, and to try again after failing is hard-wired into our DNA as human beings. Sadly, many schools and educators consciously or unconsciously attempt to "cure" children of this desire to create and make.

---

[24] Rith, C. (2007, January 23). What 50 pounds of clay can teach you about design. LifeClever: Career Advice, Productivity Tips, and Life Hacks for Designers. Retrieved June 21, 2011, from http:// www.lifeclever.com/what-50-pounds-of-clay-can-teach-you-about-design/

In his challenging book, "Coloring Outside the Lines: Raising A Smarter Kid by Breaking All the Rules," Roger Shank offers an interesting definition of creativity relevant to our discussion about playing with media.

> A while back I wrote a book called The Creative Attitude. In it, I defined creativity as a willingness to come up with and pursue one hundred ideas knowing that ninety-nine of them are stupid. If you examine the history of creative and inventive people, you'll find that almost all of them had ninety-nine dumb ideas before they hit on one great concept. The creative attitude is having the chutzpah not to be defeated by the naysayers who put down your ideas. In other words, you need to keep plugging away. Schools (and the workplace, for that matter) don't encourage kids to voice and experiment with all their ideas. When kids receive verbal criticism from teachers and bad grades or barbed remarks from fellow students, it shuts down their creativity. Parents can counter this effect by encouraging children to pursue whatever odd and doomed-to-fail notions they may have. Be prepared for a lot of wacky ideas. No matter how strange they might be, don't discourage your child by calling his idea "weird" or "wrong." If he is dead set on building a toy house from blocks that you know is going to fall down, don't say, "This isn't going to work." Get down on the floor, help him, and when the house does fall down encourage him to try a different approach. When he sees that nothing awful happens when his idea fails,

he'll be willing to try again. This is the source
of true creativity.[25]

I anticipate many of you reading this book are professional
educators, so this call to engage in creative play with media for the
sake of creativity itself may seem like heresy... especially in our
political season of high stakes testing. For those who doubt our need
to engage in creative play with media, my best suggestion is for you
to spend time PERSONALLY creating with some of the tools and
strategies suggested in this book. We learn deeper when we actively
DO rather than passively WATCH. Creative play, with media and
with other things, is an intrinsically valuable activity which results in
tangible as well as intangible benefits. Can creative play enhance
formal assessment processes and help students meet grade level
academic expectations? Of course. It can do far more, however, and
the most important benefits which result from creative play are likely
NOT measured on a standardized test bubblesheet.

Academic Standards

The educational standards movement in the United States has
influenced K-12 school curricula and activities since "A Nation at
Risk" was published in 1983.[26] Thousands of standards have been
published by state departments of education and educational
associations. Passage of "No Child Left Behind" legislation in 2001
further cemented an educational focus in most public schools in the
USA on standards-based education. In Oklahoma, where I live with

---

[25] Schank, R. C. (2000). Coloring outside the lines: raising a smarter
kid by breaking all the rules. New York: HarperCollinsPublishers.
Pages 33-34.

[26] Phelan, R. (2003, January 23). Overview of the Standards
Movement. Special Education 423B. Retrieved June 21, 2011, from
http://www.sonoma.edu/users/p/phelan/423/standards.html

my family, we presently have over 3000 different standards for students enrolled in K-12 public schools. The standards movement has had and maintains some laudable goals, including increased expectations for student achievement in our communities. Unfortunately, however, the standards movement along with high stakes testing policies has encouraged educators in many schools to abandon project based learning approaches as well as assignments which involve student choice and creativity.

The Common Core State Standards Initiative (www.corestandards.org) is an effort to simplify and streamline the landscape of educational standards in the United States. According to the mission statement of Common Core:

> The Common Core State Standards provide a consistent, clear understanding of what students are expected to learn, so teachers and parents know what they need to do to help them. The standards are designed to be robust and relevant to the real world, reflecting the knowledge and skills that our young people need for success in college and careers. With American students fully prepared for the future, our communities will be best positioned to compete successfully in the global economy.[27]

While all states in the United States have not adopted Common Core as of this writing, the operational goal of simplifying and clarifying high expectations for student learning inside and outside our school classrooms is a good one all communities should embrace. Media technologies are essential elements of literacy and communication in the 21st century. The Common Core Initiative

---

[27] Common Core State Standards Initiative. (n.d.). Common Core State Standards Initiative. Retrieved June 21, 2011, from http://www.corestandards.org

supports the integrated use of technologies throughout its standards for students to not only access media content, but also create media. According to the Initiative's about page:

> Just as media and technology are integrated in school and life in the twenty-first century, skills related to media use (both critical analysis and production of media) are integrated throughout the standards.[28]

Educators focused on meeting state academic standards in the Common Core, therefore, are "right at home" playing with media and seeking to better understand the ways media creation can be used to support student learning. A variety of other academic standards adopted by states and schools also focus on the importance of technology integration, including media/content creation.

The definition of 21st century literacies adopted by the National Council of Teachers of English (NCTE) in 1998 is filled with references to visual literacy and media literacy. The NCTE Framework for 21st Century Curriculum and Assessment REQUIRES students to create multimedia texts.[29] Twenty-first century readers and writers are required, by the standards, to:

> Develop proficiency with the tools of technology
>
> Build relationships with others to pose and solve problems collaboratively and cross-culturally

---

[28] About: Common Core State Standards Initiative | Key Points. (n.d.). Common Core State Standards Initiative. Retrieved June 21, 2011, from http://www.corestandards.org/about-the-standards/key-points-in-english-language-arts

[29] 21st Century Literacies. (n.d.). National Council of Teachers of English - Homepage . Retrieved June 21, 2011, from http://www.ncte.org/governance/literacies

Design and share information for global communities to meet a variety of purposes

Manage, analyze, and synthesize multiple streams of simultaneous information

Create, critique, analyze, and evaluate multimedia texts

Attend to the ethical responsibilities required by these complex environments

The National Educational Technology Standards (NETS) for Students also require "playing with media," although those specific words are a paraphrase. The first of six standards, Creativity and Innovation, requires that "students demonstrate creative thinking, construct knowledge, and develop innovative products and processes using technology."[30] Students cannot meet the NETS-S by simply browsing the web, watching videos, and conducting research. Students must actively create with media. We learn to effectively create with media, as previously discussed in the section on "Creativity," by playing with media.

The skills required to "play with media" are not simply the domain of technology and English teachers, however. To be literate in our society, individuals should understand not only the power of visual images, but also be able to create and share digital stories which communicate ideas, relay emotions, and archive history. Michael Wesch, professor of cultural anthropology at Kansas State University and renowned for several viral YouTube videos he has co-created with his students, contends we cannot be fully "media literate" today unless we understand how to create and share multimedia messages effectively. Shifting our schools and our educational systems beyond the dissemination or "delivery" of

---

[30] Society for Technology in Education. (n.d.). NETS for Students. ISTE | NETS Standards. Retrieved June 21, 2011, from http://www.iste.org/standards/nets-for-students.aspx

information to students is challenging, but is a goal we must each find ways to tangibly advance. It is vital as educators we seek to empower students to become fully literate, and this requires us to all become media CREATORS rather than mere consumers.

Additional thoughts related to the "why" of Playing with Media are available in the appendix: Thoughts on the Attention Economy.

2- Digital Text

iPad Text by Rachel Fryer [31]

Words are powerful.

For quick proof, ask a young person with a cell phone text messaging plan about a hurtful text message they have received or read that a friend received. Words do not have to be published in books or magazines to be both powerful and impactful. The digital screens now at our fingertips, including cell phones, laptops, touch-tablets, and other devices offer more opportunities to share more text with more people than ever in human history. How are we helping young people learn to both respect and constructively utilize the

---

[31] Fryer, R. (2011, June 21). Text by Rachel Fryer. Flickr - Photo Sharing. Retrieved July 22, 2011, from http://www.flickr.com/photos/wfryer/5875726712/in/set-72157626886284140

power of digital text now at their fingertips? The focus of this chapter is "digital text," and finding ways as educators to leverage digital writing platforms safely and effectively with students inside and outside the classroom.

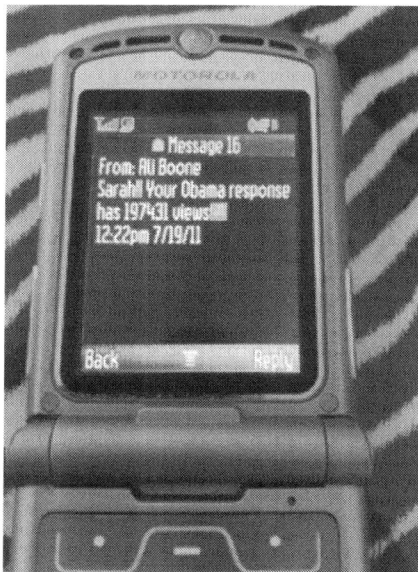

SMS Message [32]

Blog or Wiki?

Here is a quick activity to get us started: You have sixty seconds. Turn to someone near you and either explain or ask them to explain the difference between a "blog" and a "wiki." These are both terms utilized extensively when we discuss online, interactive writing today.

---

[32] Fryer, A. (2011, July 23). SMS Message. Welcome to Flickr - Photo Sharing. Retrieved July 23, 2011, from http://www.flickr.com/photos/wfryer/5968292848/

Yet frequently when I visit with educators, many are unsure how to define these terms and differentiate between them.

Both wikis and blogs are websites which can be readily edited using a web browser. Special software is not required to create and publish digital text on these platforms. There are important differences between them, however.

Think of a blog like a digital newspaper. Consider the New York Times. Each day, headlines on the paper's website change. Past articles are "archived" on the website, but may not be readily viewable and linked on the initial homepage of the site. Articles are time and date stamped, so visitors can readily learn when a particular article was posted as well as the name of the author who wrote it. These characteristics generally define "blogs" as well. Some people still think of "blogs" primarily as websites which are personal diaries. While some people certainly use blogs as diaries, that definition falls far short of defining "blogs" as a platform. The primarily feature which defines a blog as different from another website is the time and date stamp associated with each "post" on the site, and GENERALLY the display of most recent posts on the front page or homepage of a blog site.

Think of a wiki like an encyclopedia. WikiPedia is one of the most famous websites in the world which uses "wiki software" (MediaWiki) as its underlying platform "powering" the site. Each page on a wiki has a "history" which users can access to view and compare changes made on the site. Each time a wiki page changes, an archived version of the page is saved along with the date, time, and username of the individual who made the change.

Revision history of Transmediation

From Wikipedia, the free encyclopedia

English WikiPedia History of Transmediation [33]

If anonymous edits are permitted on the <u>wiki</u> (which varies by page on WikiPedia) the IP address of the computer used to make the change is logged. This format makes wikis great digital spaces to build documents together.

For many classes and classrooms, it makes sense for teachers and students to use both a <u>blog</u> (or multiple blogs) and a wiki for information sharing and collaboration. Since blogs and wikis have different characteristics, they can meet different needs and solve different problems.

---

[33] History of Transmediation Page. (n.d.). English WikiPedia. Retrieved July 22, 2011, from <u>http://en.wikipedia.org/w/index.php?title=Transmediation&action=history</u>

Wikis as Class Information Portals

Educators utilizing technology tools need an "information portal" or "home base" to use with students, parents, teachers, and other members of the community.[34] This webpage or website can be used by students, parents, and others to regularly access news, links, and other digital content shared by the teacher. In many cases, a publicly-accessible wiki site can meet this need better than other types of websites. While many universities and an increasing number of K-12 schools utilize LMS ("learning management system") platforms like Moodle, Blackboard/WebCT, Sakai, etc., those LMS sites generally require users to login for access and are examples of "closed web" rather than "open web" publishing platforms.

Moodle Login for UNT Learning Technologies [35]

---

[34] Henderson, M. (2011). Quoted on the blog post, Managing iOS Devices in the Classroom. Moving at the Speed of Creativity. Retrieved June 22, 2011, from http://www.speedofcreativity.org/2011/06/10/managing-ios-devices-in-the-classroom-tatc11/

[35] Moodle Login. (n.d.). University of North Texas Learning Technologies. Retrieved July 22, 2011, from http://moodle.lt.unt.edu

While confidential information like student grades, attendance data, and tests/quizzes should sensibly be shared on password-protected LMS websites, **the vast majority of curricular links, assignments, and announcements shared by teachers with their classroom community can and should be shared on "open web" sites like wikis.** Collaboration and creativity hinge on the ability to build on the ideas of others, so when teachers "lock up" course content behind a password-protected login they rob the rest of the world of the opportunity to learn from and with them. Open web publishing for as much non-confidential content as possible is a digital ethic we need to follow as twenty-first century educators.

Two examples of outstanding classroom wikis utilized as "information portals" or "home base" websites were created by primary grade teachers on opposite sides of the world. One teacher was inspired to create her site after seeing the other teacher's site and presentation in the free, K-12 Online Conference. Rachel Boyd is a primary years teacher and school administrator in New Zealand. Her Room 9 Classroom wiki, room9nelsoncentral.wikispaces.com, is an exemplary "home base" or information portal website. Rachel shared how she used this website with her students and parents in her twenty minute keynote presentation, "A Peek for a Week – Inside a Kiwi Junior Classroom" for K12Online.

Room 9 Nelson Central's LEARNING HUB by Rachel Boyd [36]

Rachel Boyd's classroom wiki inspired Maria Knee, a kindergarten teacher in Deerfield, New Hampshire, to create her classroom "home base" wiki, The KinderKids Learning on thekinderkids.wikispaces.com.

---

[36] Boyd, R. (2009). Room 9 Nelson Central's Learning Hub. Retrieved June 22, 2011, from http:// room9nelsoncentral.wikispaces.com

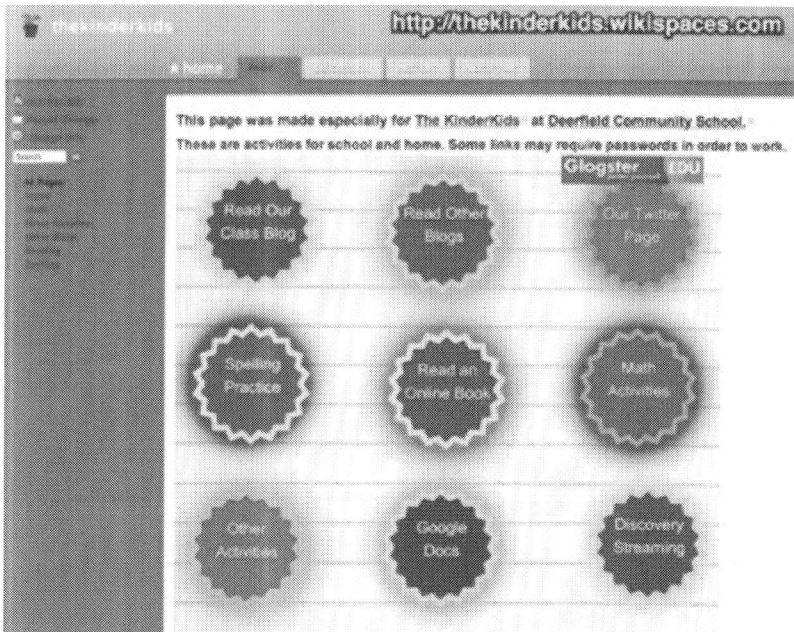

The Kinderkids by Maria Knee [37]

Both Rachel and Maria's classroom learning portal websites are hosted for free on wikispaces.com. Wikispaces is an excellent wiki platform for classroom teachers to utilize, and provides free, ad-free wikis to educators worldwide via the page, www.wikispaces.com/content/for/teachers.

Do not think, because both of these class information portal websites are used by primary years teachers, that this type of educational wiki use is not for teachers of older students. It is relevant for teachers at all levels. In teaching university pre-service education students, I've used free wiki sites hosted by Google Sites (sites.google.com) for my course curriculum, in conjunction with each institution's respective learning management system.

---

[37] Knee, M. (2011.). The KinderKids Learning Page. Retrieved July 22, 2011, from http://thekinderkids.wikispaces.com

Technology 4 Teachers Course Website by Wesley Fryer [38]

Consider using a <u>wiki</u>-based website as an "information learning portal" or "home base" for your own students. Since each edited version of a wiki is automatically archived, it's generally easy to "revert" a mistakenly edited or saved page to a previous, "good" version. Every classroom teacher should not only understand how wiki websites work, but also be able to proficiently add text, hyperlinks, images, and embedded <u>rich media</u> (like videos) to a wiki.

Wikis are powerful and we need to utilize them in our classrooms, but they are GENERALLY not as simple and fast to use as <u>blogs</u>. Numerous web-based resources are available to help you learn how to utilize wikis effectively in the classroom. Two I recommend (which are both free) are <u>Paula White</u>'s K12Online

---

[38] Fryer, W. (2011). Technology 4 Teachers by Wesley Fryer. Retrieved June 22, 2011, from <u>http://wiki.wesfryer.com/t4t</u>

presentation, "Parallel Play or Collaboration–Leveraging the Wiki Platform for High Quality Work" and Mark Wagner's K12Online presentation, "Wiki While You Work (Basic.)" [39] [40]

Blogs as Interactive Sharing Spaces

Every classroom needs a blog. Relative to other available platforms for sharing digital content today, a blog can provide the fastest way to interactively share rich media while permitting the teacher(s) the ability to MODERATE content shared on the blog site before it becomes publicly visible for anyone online to see. This assertion requires several definitions of terms.

interactively share: A website supporting "interactive sharing" permits different users to submit and contribute content, as well as reply / respond to the submissions of others. If your website isn't interactive today, it was either created with 20th century web design tools or created BY individuals still locked in 20th century modes of thinking about digital content. Interactive sharing is an essential part of every leading website online today. If your website is not "interactive" by this definition, you need to build a new one.

rich media: Rich media content can include digital text, hyperlinks to other online resources, images, embedded audio files, videos, and other forms of digital animation. Websites which do not permit the embedding and sharing of rich media elements (to create an online "compound document," as defined in WikiPedia) are

---

[39] Wagner, M. (2006). Basic/Advanced Training: Wiki While You Work. The K12 Online Conference. Retrieved June 22, 2011, from http://k12onlineconference.org/?p=53

[40] White, P. (2009). Parallel Play or Collaboration–Leveraging the Wiki Platform for High Quality Work. The K12 Online Conference. Retrieved June 22, 2011, from http://k12onlineconference.org/?p=576

disabled or crippled, relative to sites which do.[41] "Playing with media," in my view, must extend beyond simple text-based sharing into the realm of rich media.

moderate content: Content moderation is the process of reviewing and either approving or rejecting submitted content to be publicly viewed on a website. For classroom blogs, teachers should serve as content moderators. In our litigious US society, the reasons for this should be clear. No one wants to utilize an interactive website and offend students, parents, administrators, or others in the community with content posted to the site. Content moderation is the process of "gatekeeping" website content so offensive, inappropriate, or otherwise undesirable media is not publicly shown to others. While classroom teachers in some circumstances (and locations) may want to utilize different levels of content moderation, the CAPABILITY to moderate content is an essential requirement for any blog used by a classroom teacher.

While there are numerous blog platforms available today, one blogging platform is transformatively simple because it is based on email and email attachments: Posterous.com. Posterous was founded by two young men who wanted to enable their parents, in their 60s, to be able to share rich media content online using email.[42] Since most educators in the United States are both familiar and comfortable using email and email attachments, Posterous is an ideal,

---

[41] Compound document. (n.d.). Wikipedia, the free encyclopedia. Retrieved June 4, 2011, from http://en.wikipedia.org/wiki/Compound_document. Note my use of this term does not strictly comply with the definition provided by WikiPedia or the W3C.

[42] Fryer, W. (2010). How We're Reinventing the Blog by Sachin Agarwal (Posterous co-founder.) Moving at the Speed of Creativity. Retrieved June 22, 2011, from http://www.speedofcreativity.org/2010/05/12/how-were-reinventing-the-blog-by-sachin-agarwal-posterous-co-founder/

FREE website for classroom teachers to use for safely sharing content interactively online.

The Ethic of Minimal Clicks

The word "easy" should be used sparingly in the context of communication technologies. Something which is "easy" or obvious for one person might seem hopelessly complicated to another, especially if the latter individual is not familiar with basic terms and concepts relevant to the task under consideration. In my work with educators at all levels since the mid 1990s, I have noticed the "number of clicks" (or "gestures" on a touch device, as the case may be) makes a HUGE difference in whether a new technology skill is adopted by a novice learner. The complexity of a technology-based task can be directly measured by the number of "clicks" it takes to perform. Something which takes a few clicks (like creating and sending a new email message) is much more likely to become a ubiquitous skill. Something which takes ten or twenty clicks, on the other hand, is likely to be adopted by only a handful of innovator or early-adopter users. The bell shaped curve and familiar labels of the "technology adoption lifecycle," shown below, was developed as a sociological model by Joe M. Bohlen, George M. Beal and Everett M. Rogers. This applies to groups of teachers using technology in most schools, just as it did to farmers willing to purchase "high tech" hybrid corn seed in the midwest in the 1950s when the model was created.[43]

---

[43] Technology adoption lifecycle. (n.d.). Wikipedia, the free encyclopedia. Retrieved June 23, 2011, from http://en.wikipedia.org/wiki/Technology_adoption_lifecycle

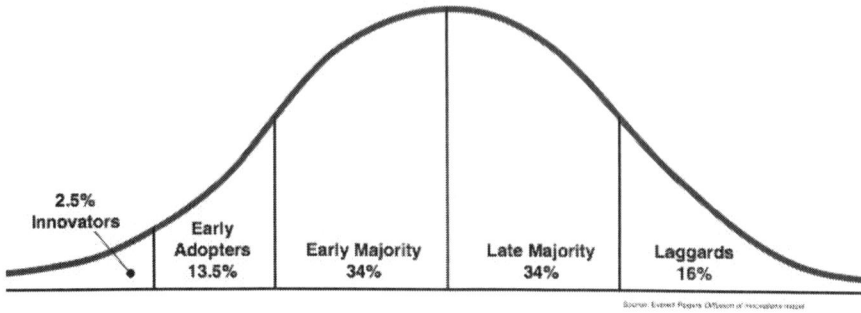

The Technology Adoption Lifecycle from the English WikiPedia

When it comes to technology integration in our schools and "playing with media," we do NOT want to restrict these activities to a limited group of innovators and early adopters. Rather, we want ALL teachers (even the "laggards") to adopt and utilize media technologies effectively to support learning. Given this goal, the "ethic of minimal clicks" is crucial to understand and embrace. Uses of technology which require fewer clicks can be naturally adopted by a larger percentage of educators than those which are more complex and cumbersome. **Digital simplicity matters.**

The "ethic of minimal clicks" is a big reason Posterous can be a transformative tool for sharing digital text and other forms of rich media with students in your classroom.

Quicksharing with Posterous

Disclosure: I do NOT have any ties to Posterous.com, the company's founders, employees, nor investors. I'm a Posterous user, but do not have another agenda in endorsing them other than my belief that they've created one of the simplest, easiest, and most powerful platforms for rich media sharing. I am on a continuing quest for tools which support the "ethic of minimal clicks," and Posterous definitely fits that bill.

Posterous Basics

There are two ways to get started sharing digital text and rich media with a free blog on Posterous.com.

1. Send an email to post@posterous.com. A blog will automatically be created which is connected to your email address, and the content of your email message (including any attached media files) will be included in your first post on the blog.

2. Visit the website posterous.com and create a free account by entering your email address, a username you want, and your desired password. The username you select will become your first Posterous site address subdomain: username.posterous.com.

To create a classroom blog on Posterous, you'll most likely want to create a SITE rather than a GROUP when prompted after creating your account.

These days, Posterous comes in two flavors:

The original. It's the easiest way to share anything with anyone: across the room, or around the world.

Now it's easier than ever to foster great conversations. A group is like an email list on steroids.

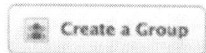

Once your site is created, anytime you want to create a new post you can simply send an email to Posterous. The subject line of your email message will become the title of the blog post, and any rich media files you attach to the email will also be included in your post. Some kinds of media will be given special treatment by Posterous.

1. Images will be embedded in the post, so visitors can see them without clicking a link on the post. If you attach more than one image to an email sent to Posterous, the site will create a clickable image gallery on your post which visitors can view.

2. Direct links to videos on YouTube, as well as several other video sharing sites like Vimeo, will "auto-embed" on your post. This means like images, they will display as embedded media visitors can simply view in your post and watch by clicking the play button. You do NOT have to copy special "embed code" from the video sharing website hosting each video: Posterous

automatically makes the videos appear as embedded versions. Attached word processing files are automatically converted to Scribd.com "embeddable" documents.

You can use different email addresses when posting media to Posterous depending on how you want your content posted and shared.

1. Email to post@posterous.com to post the content directly on your designated "main" Posterous blog, AND (if configured) "auto-post" content to other websites you've specified.

2. Email to posterous@posterous.com to post content directly on your designated "main" Posterous blog but NOT "auto-post" content to configured third-party sites.

3. Email to yourblogusername@posterous.com (where "yourblogusername" is the username you selected for the blog to which you want to post) to BOTH publish content directly on your site and "auto-post" to configured third-party sites.

Option three above functions the same as option one, except other people can also use that email address if you choose to allow them to post to your Posterous blog. This is the method you can use to allow students to directly post content (including rich media) to your class Posterous blog. To do this, after logging into your Posterous account you'll want to select your blog and click SETTINGS.

Next, click to EDIT settings for Commenting and Posting.

Choose the options:

1. Anyone can post, I will moderate

2. Anyone can comment

3. Moderate comments (check this checkbox)

After making these initial configuration changes, your free, class blog on Posterous.com is ready for students (or others) to submit content which won't "go live" on your site until you approve it. Changing these Posterous blog settings so posts as well as comments are moderated is an essential step, but once it's been completed you shouldn't have to repeat it unless you setup another free Posterous site. To do that you don't need to create another account, you simply need to choose "Create a New One" below your list of Posterous sites in the left sidebar of the website.

The eleven minute screencast on YouTube, "Set up a Moderated Class Blog on Posterous," demonstrates these setup procedures as well as how you can moderate submitted posts. This is also shared, with additional "backstory" information, on the PlayingWithMedia.com site. Procedures for configuring "auto-posting" to other third party websites (like another blog, a class Twitter account, etc.) from Posterous are also addressed.[44] Unlike the other screencasts created for this eBook project using the free website Screenr.com, this screencast was created with the commercial screencasting program Screenflow.

Examples of Educational Posterous Blogs Using Digital Text

Before exploring some technical but relevant aspects of blogs like those created on Posterous.com, let's explore a few examples of educational Posterous blogs. Using email to post rich media to a Posterous blog can be very empowering, and enable students of all ages to readily collaborate online in ways which might be more difficult to share otherwise. Since this chapter focuses on sharing and playing with "digital text," Posterous examples included here are mainly text-based. In the chapter on "Images" there are examples of Posterous blogs used for image sharing.

Level 1: Broadcast Sharing (An assignment blog)

One of the first ways many teachers start using a blog with students is to post assignments. This is an important and exciting first

---

[44] Fryer, W. (2011). Set up a Moderated Class Blog on Posterous. YouTube - Broadcast Yourself. Retrieved June 23, 2011, from http://www.youtube.com/watch?v=Pf17216KpL0

step for many teachers to publish digital information online. Julie Eisenband of Sage Academy in Minnesota created a blog titled "AP World History" to share (among other things) homework assignments for students.[45]

Eddie Thompson, an elementary teacher in Ohio, has used two Posterous blogs for his students and parents. One blog, "Mr. Thompson's Homework," is used to strictly post homework

---

[45] Eisenband, J. (2010). AP World History - Class Web site for students of SAGE Academy. Posterous.com. Retrieved June 23, 2011, from http://jeeapwh.posterous.com

assignments each week.[46] He has used a second Posterous blog, "Mr. Thompson's Classroom Blog," to publish announcements and updates for parents and students. Thompson's use of digital tools extends beyond blogs to include a classroom wiki, social bookmarking site, Twitter account, and Skype account.[47] His growing "digital footprint" of interactive websites utilized for student/parent communication, professional growth and student interaction sets a good example. Teachers acquire the knowledge and skills to utilize technology resources like these over time, but often this journey begins with the use of an assignment blog. Do not underestimate the importance of what may appear (to some) to be a minor act, like creating a Posterous blog for assignment sharing. Every great journey begins with a single step.

Level 2: A Professional Reflection Blog

A growing number of teachers around the world are using blogs to reflect on their teaching and learning. The value of continually reflecting on our teaching practice as educators is well documented and is integrated into the process of National Board Certification in the United States.[48] Jim Peterson, a high school physics teacher in

---

[46] Thompson, E. (n.d.). Mr. Thompson's Homework - Home. Posterous.com. Retrieved June 23, 2011, from http:// mrthompsonsclassroomhomework.posterous.com

[47] Thompson, E. (n.d.). Mr. Thompson's Second Grade Class - Contacts. Retrieved June 23, 2011, from http:// www.mrthompsonsclassroom.com/contacts

[48] Profile of Professional Growth. (n.d.). National Board for Professional Teaching Standards: National Board for Professional Teaching Standards. Retrieved June 23, 2011, from http:// www.nbpts.org/for_nbcts/certification_renewal/ profile_of_professional

Holland, Michigan, uses a Posterous blog to share reflections and in his words, "document my learning journey."[49]

Professional reflection blogs are online spaces which not only help the authors grow, they also can help many other educators around the world learn. I personally subscribe to hundreds of educator blogs like these within an "education" category in my Google Reader account. You can view this linked list on www.speedofcreativity.org/resources/education-blogs, and subscribe to these blogs (if you want a jump-start on your own education blog

---

[49] Peterson, J. (n.d.). Jim's posterous - Explore... Discover.... Retrieved June 23, 2011, from http://weathertation.posterous.com

subscriptions) by linking to these blogs shared as a Google Reader "bundle."[50]

While many different blog platform options are available today, Posterous is a free, flexible, and easy-to use option which should be considered by educators looking for online spaces to support their digital sharing.

Level 3: A Collaborative Class Blog

Whether you are teaching a classroom of adults or young students, it can be challenging to digitally collect or "aggregate" ideas shared by your students during and after class. Learning Management Systems (LMS'es) like Moodle and Blackboard, as previously mentioned, can address this need. LMS sites are NOT public, however, and because they are on the "closed web" they should NOT be the exclusive spaces where we share ideas and publish information from our classrooms. Open web publishing and sharing empowers creativity and collaboration in ways closed web publishing never will.

Tim Bray, a high school language arts teacher and technology integration specialist in South Korea, uses a Posterous blog to not only share assignments for his students but also showcase their work. (kis-world-literature.posterous.com) Tim uses the tag "studentwork" to identify posts on the blog which include student media products.

---

[50] Fryer, W. (2011). Education Blogs Subscriptions. Google Reader. Retrieved June 23, 2011, from http://www.google.com/reader/bundle/user/04501019582704505857/bundle/education

Some of these documents are posted to the website Scribd.com and then embedded on the blog, like the cartoon project below.[51]

In a recent workshop with Texas elementary school principals learning to use iPads, I used a Posterous blog titled "Edu-Sandbox" (edusandbox.posterous.com) to collect responses to the four-minute video, "Montana Voices: Digital Vision for Schools 2011 Challenge" and question: What does it mean to have "digital vision"

---

[51] Bray, T. (2011). World Literature - Filed under 'student work'. World Literature - KIS 9th World Literature Blog. Retrieved June 24, 2011, from http://kis-world-literature.posterous.com/? tag=studentwork

as a school leader today?[52] This is one of the responses from a workshop participant.

Edu Sandbox

a media sandbox for co-learners

« Back to blog

Jun 15 | **Ideas about digital leadership from Southwest ISD**

Ideas about digital leadership from Southwest ISD

It is up to the leaders to lead by example and provide the support for teachers to feel safe in trying new things. We need to send the message that that we cannot wait to become the experts before we expose our students to technology. Our students are ready. They cannot wait for all of us to be ready.

It is imperative that student learning through and with technology become the norm. Teachers must be expected to facilitate this learning and as leaders we must provide the support in terms of training and resources.

Angelica Romero
Principal of Medio Creek

🐦 Tweet   0   👍 Like

2 responses   ♥   💬

♥ Kathy Schrock liked this post.   5 days ago

💬 Scott Laleman responded: 4 days ago

> I agree with most of what you've said, but I think that teachers do need to have some level of comfort with technology before it is introduced to their students. The teacher needs to know what to expect, and have a backup plan in case the technology doesn't work well. It also doesn't hurt to have extra help on hand (in the form of an Instructional Technologist) who can help troubleshoot if something goes wrong. That way, the teacher can focus on teaching the content.

http://edusandbox.posterous.com/ideas-about-digital-leadership-from-southwest

---

[52] Fryer, W. (2011). Montana Voices: Digital Vision for Schools 2011 Challenge .YouTube - Broadcast Yourself.. Retrieved February 7, 2011, from http://www.youtube.com/watch?v=8QB64yZBLMc

Often in face-to-face classes, there is not sufficient time to give each student an opportunity to share his/her responses to a discussion prompt. By utilizing a Posterous site as a collaboration platform, however, each student can type a response and email their text to a Posterous site email address. After the teacher moderates and approves submitted posts, everyone in the class or workshop can view the ideas of others and comment on them.

This type of spontaneous, interactive, collaborative digital work is exactly the kind of communication exchanges which blogs can and should empower in our classrooms. Hopefully by seeing these examples of Posterous blogs in action, used by teachers and students in different ways, you can better understand the power and potential of this blogging platform.

Adding Links to Posterous Posts

Hyperlinks are one of the most important things learners need to be able to use with digital texts. Just as words are powerful, hyperlinks are powerful too. The ability to connect words to website text, images, audio and video is a skill which would have been considered "magical" in previous centuries. Hypertext websites, like blogs and wikis, provide visitors opportunities to extend their learning about different topics by using links. When writing and sharing blog posts, try to use relevant hyperlinks frequently.

There are two basic ways to add hyperlinks to a Posterous blog post:

1. Paste the full URL (web address) of the website you want to share onto a new line in your blog post. Hyperlinks can be inserted in this way when web-posting to a Posterous blog or when posting by email.

2. If web-posting to a Posterous blog, users can highlight text they want to make into a hyperlink and then use the link tool to paste the URL and save it as a hyperlink.

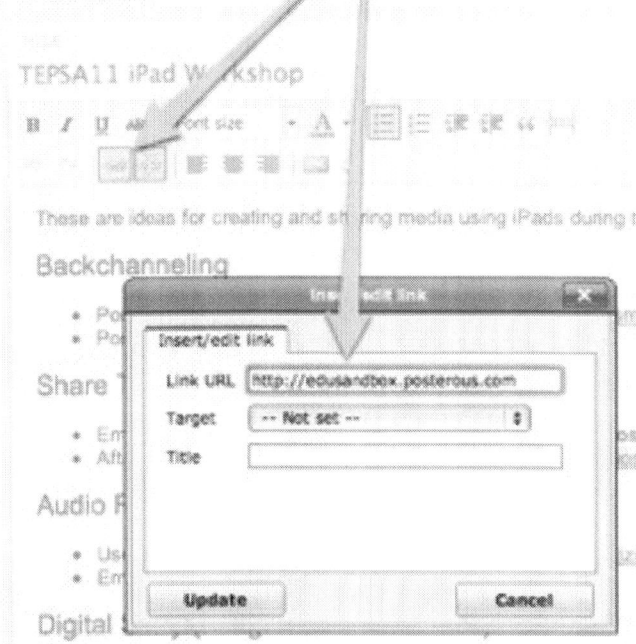

Use the link tool (it looks like a chain) to insert hyperlinks in Posterous Posts

As previously mentioned, however, Posterous is specially configured to "auto-embed" links to certain websites, like YouTube. The example below is a post I shared during a recent workshop, and includes a YouTube video link.

TITLE

Ideas about Digital Leadership from Wes

B *I* U ABC | Font size ▾ | A ▾ | ≡ ≡ ≡ ≡ 66 ⋈

Ideas about Digital Leadership from Wes

These are ideas about digitally informed leadership in schools, inspired in part by this video:

http://www.youtube.com/watch?v=8QB64yZBLMc

Sent from my iPad

Posterous blog auto-embed example for a YouTube video

Because of Posterous' auto-embed functionality, this blog post appears with the full video embedded into the post in the publicly viewable version.

Edu Sandbox

a media sandbox for co-learners

« Back to blog

JUN 15 Ideas about Digital Leadership from Wes

Ideas about Digital Leadership from Wes

These are ideas about digitally informed leadership in schools, inspired in part by this video:

Montana Voices: Digital Vision for Schools 2011...

Sent from my iPad

Tweet 0 Like

Other blogging platforms, like Wordpress, also support auto-embedding of YouTube video links in more recent versions.

Other Technical Blog Stuff

Web Browsers

In some cases, I've found Google Chrome (www.google.com/chrome) and Mozilla Firefox (getfirefox.com) function better with web-based blog sites than versions of the Internet Explorer browser.[53] I recommend readers of this book use Chrome and/or Firefox as their primary web browser(s). These browsers often operate faster than Internet Explorer. Apple's Safari web browser (www.apple.com/safari) is another free option. It synchronizes its bookmarks to iOS devices like an iPhone or iPad. Like other digital tools discussed in this book, I encourage readers to play with various web browsers on your computer to get a personal sense of the differences and relative benefits between them. It's critical to understand and teach others: Internet Explorer is NOT "the only game in town" when it comes to web browsers.

---

[53] Fryer, W. (2010, December 21). Lessons Learned Teaching EdTech to PreService Education Students (Fall 2010). Moving at the Speed of Creativity. Retrieved June 24, 2011, from http://www.speedofcreativity.org/2010/12/21/lessons-learned-teaching-edtech-to-preservice-education-students-fall-2010/

Two Faces of a Blog: Public and Private

Unlike a wiki, which can permit users to directly edit pages of the website, blogs are edited from a "dashboard" or private view. Think of a blog as having two FACES: the "public" face / version which visitors to the site see, and the "private" face / version which those with editing "rights" can see and change. These public and private "faces" of a blog site are present in every online blogging platform I've used to date. Each web-based blog has a special link administrators and contributors can use to login to the "private" face or dashboard. In the case of a Posterous site, users simply login at Posterous.com. For a Wordpress site, generally the suffix "wp-admin" is added after the domain name of the blog to access the dashboard. Some blogs will have a link which says "admin" or "login" for this purpose. It's important to use secure passwords for your blog sites, and change them frequently, since this is the best insurance to protect against someone hacking into your site.

Cloud Computing: Client versus Web-Based Blogs

Most blogs today are powered by "content management system" software which runs on an Internet server. These are web-based blogs, and they can be edited (generally) with any Internet-connected computer using any web browser. Posterous.com, Wordpress.com, and Blogger.com are all examples of web-based blogs.

Some blogs, however, are created and updated with client-based software which generally runs on a single computer. iWeb by Apple (www.apple.com/ilife/iweb/) is an example of a client-based blogging software program, as is Thingamablog (www.thingamablog.com). (This reference is just for you, Miguel!) While some client-side blogging software programs provide greater design options for blog and website creators not familiar with CSS and HTML coding (check out the iterations of Kevin Honeycutt's professional website for examples) these websites are inherently limited because they do not fully "live in the cloud."

Cloud computing refers to website based applications which run entirely over the Internet.[54]

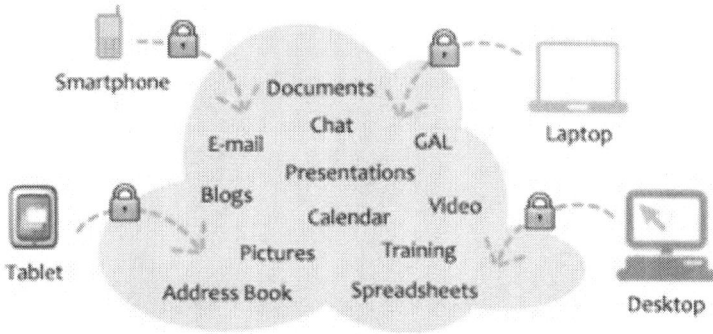

Cloud Computing

Having secure access to all your applications and data from any network device

When a web-based blogging platform is used to create a website, content on that website can be updated from multiple devices rather than a single computer running a special software program. As an example, Posterous has free smartphone applications for iPhone/iOS users (posterous.com/mobile/iphone) as well as Android users (posterous.com/mobile/android.) Blog authors using Wordpress can also utilize a free application for iOS devices (ios.wordpress.org.)

---

[54] Cloud computing. (n.d.). Wikipedia, the free encyclopedia. Retrieved June 24, 2011, from http://en.wikipedia.org/wiki/Cloud_computing

Multiple cloud-based blogging platforms, including Blogger.com, are supported by the commercial iOS application Blog Press (blogpressapp.com). As we move further into a computing environment dominated by mobile devices, the kind of multi-device access provided by web-based blogging platforms will only increase in utility.

Other Blog Platform Recommendations

While Posterous.com is my primary recommended blog site for you as you begin to "play with media" and share digital text, there certainly are other blogging platforms which deserve mention for possible use as a class blog.

As of this writing, Kidblog.org is my top recommendation for teachers looking to start an interactive class blog in addition to Posterous. Kidblog is very "Wordpress-like" in its dashboard interface for posting, and I like the homepage layout of each Kidblog site. The screenshot below is from one of my pre-service education class blogs.[55]

---

[55] Fryer, W. (2011). T4T Spring 2011 Fryer - 11 am. Kidblog.org - Blogs for Teachers and Students. Retrieved June 24, 2011, from http://kidblog.org/T4TSpring2011Fryer/

Kidblog:

1. Is completely free, regardless of how many students you have in class

2. Is completely advertisement free

3. Automatically makes a nice blog directory in the right sidebar of your homepage

4. Shows visitors how many (or how few) comments recent blog posts have received

Class Blogmeister (classblogmeister.com) is another free, ad-free blogging platform designed specifically for classroom use by David

Warlick. Kindergarten teacher Maria Knee, who I highlighted previously for her superb classroom wiki, configures her personal domain (mariaknee.com) to forward directly to her current class's blog on Classroom Blogmeister. Maria and her students do a commendable job sharing their activities and learning journey each year on their blog. Notice in the screenshot below how Class Blogmeister also creates a nice directory of student blogs in the right sidebar, and also separates teacher entries from student entries in the left sidebar.

The KinderKids' Blog by Maria Knee [56]

[56] Knee, M. (2011). The KinderKids Blog.Landmarks Class Blogmeister. Retrieved July 23, 2011, from http://classblogmeister.com/blog.php?blogger_id=51141

Warlick designed Class Blogmeister so students could submit posts for teacher review. After the review process, the posts can "go live" on the public blog. Definitely take a close look at Class Blogmeister as well as Kidblog.org if you want to utilize a classroom blog with different features than those offered by Posterous.com.

Summary

Hopefully this discussion of tools and websites supporting "digital text sharing" has inspired you to try some new strategies with your students. Remember the power of words, the power of hyperlinks, and the power of Posterous. Utilize a free Posterous blog to aggregate and share your students' ideas, and then explore the other multimedia sharing possibilities which Posterous blogs also offer. Playing with digital text is just the beginning to our adventures playing with media.

See Appendix B: Backchannels and eBooks for additional ideas, resources and strategies about playing and creating with digital text.

3- Audio

Audio Connections by Rachel Fryer [57]

There is magical power in the human voice.

We frequently hear people say "a picture is worth a thousand words," but pictures can be worth far more to us when they can speak through an associated audio recording. The following photograph was taken at the USS Arizona Memorial (www.nps.gov/valr) in Pearl Harbor, Hawaii. This is a photo of my daughter, who

---

[57] Fryer, R. (2011, June 26). Audio by Rachel Fryer. Flickr - Photo Sharing. Retrieved July 4, 2011, from http://www.flickr.com/photos/wfryer/5875187113/in/set-72157626886284140

was five at the time, looking down into the waters below the memorial where the USS Arizona still lies.[58]

[58] Fryer, W. (2009). Rachel looks down at the USS Arizona battleship in Pearl Harbor | Flickr - Photo Sharing. Flickr - Photo Sharing. Retrieved July 14, 2009, from http://www.flickr.com/photos/wfryer/3722525388/in/set-72157623483855433/

Taken by itself, this photograph shows the shadow of something below the water and a young child looking over the railing. Combined with an audio recording made at the time, however, this photograph can "say" much more. When we were visiting the Arizona Memorial and peering down into the waters of Pearl Harbor, I asked Rachel to share some of her ideas and perceptions about what the USS Arizona is and what the memorial meant. She recorded a 97 second audio reflection using my smartphone and the free website service, AudioBoo.fm.[59]

http://audioboo.fm/boos/42836-uss-arizona-impressions

To enable readers to listen to this audio recording and learn about AudioBoo's capabilities, I recorded a 90 second screencast of

---

[59] Fryer, R. (2009, July 14). USS Arizona Impressions. Audioboo. Retrieved June 24, 2011, from http://audioboo.fm/boos/42836-uss-arizona-impressions

Rachel sharing this reflection and included some text boxes in the video highlighting some of the features as well as limitations of AudioBoo. This video is available on YouTube.[60]

Rachel's reflection about the men who died aboard the Arizona, that "their spirit went up, and their bodies went down," is both a beautiful and remarkable way for a five year old mind to express an understanding of death. Without this audio recording, we would not have any idea what was going through her young mind as she gazed down into the Hawaiian waters. Audio recordings can provide a much richer and deeper window into the thoughts, perceptions, and knowledge of our family members as well as students in our classes. I share this personal example to highlight how audio recording tools and websites can not only enhance our learning and assessment strategies in the classroom as educators, but also enrich our lives as we share our life experiences with others.

Of the digital communication options addressed in this book (digital text, audio, images and video) audio is the most under-utilized in our classrooms today. This is an unfortunate but "fixable" condition. Audio is better than video in some ways. Audio can be an extremely compelling format to document our lives as and our learning experiences for several reasons.

1. **Cameras can be intimidating**. Whether you point a still camera or a video camera in someone's face, there is an unavoidable psychological effect to that act (unless your subject is unable to see.) Microphones can still intimidate people, but generally do not elicit the same response as "being on camera." It is easier to look someone in the eye when you conduct an audio-

[60] Fryer, R. (2009, July 14). USS Arizona Impressions (AudioBoo by 5 year old Rachel) .YouTube - Broadcast Yourself. Retrieved June 24, 2011, from http://www.youtube.com/watch?v=vfT40tC2Hcs

only interview, and it is easier for them to look you in the eye if you or someone else isn't holding a camcorder. **Technology is used best for learning when it "disappears."** Audio recorders are easier to "forget" during an interview than a camera of any type. This can lead to better dialog between the interviewer and the interviewee, and therefore better digital stories.

2. **Audio recording files are comparatively small**. The smaller file sizes associated with audio recordings correspond to multiple benefits for media editors and sharers. Smaller files are faster to upload and publish online. This is especially helpful when uploading files "on the go" over slower, cell phone network (3G/4G) connections. Small files also can be edited quickly, if desired. Since they take up less space, relatively longer audio files can be stored on the same device compared to video or high resolution images. Small means "light," and even in our day of "high speed" Internet connections it can be MUCH faster to upload short audio clips to the web rather than high or medium definition videos.

3. **Audio recorders are inexpensive**. Prices certainly vary by model, but battery operated, USB-compatible digital audio recorders today can be purchased for $50 or less. Prices for video camcorders (especially point and shoot, flash-media based handheld camcorders) have come down in recent years. Most models are still over $100 unless you're looking in a pawn shop.[61] (That's a potentially good idea, by the way.)

4. **Audio recordings raise fewer privacy concerns**. Internet safety issues for young children as well as adults are real, but fears amplified by repeated "Predator Danger" television

---

[61] Fryer, W. (2011, June 4). Digital Gems in a Local Pawn Shop. Moving at the Speed of Creativity. Retrieved June 24, 2011, from http://www.speedofcreativity.org/2011/06/04/digital-gems-in-a-local-pawn-shop/

documentaries have created some unreasonable parental perceptions when it comes to sharing photos and videos online. Since audio recordings do not have to include ANY accompanying visual media (photographs or videos) the identities of students sharing audio recordings can be kept completely confidential if desired. This can be beneficial when parents are fearful about images of their child being shared online.

5. **Old and new computers can work**: The computer requirements to record, edit, and share audio are much lower than those for editing high definition video. Free and powerful software (audacity.sourceforge.net) is available for multiple computer platforms, including older systems, and the time required to import, edit, and export finished audio recordings is FAR less than it can be with video files. In many of our schools where older computer systems are the norm, this is an important benefit. Audio-based projects can be more practical and "do-able" than other kinds of media projects simply because there are fewer technical requirements.

I intentionally selected a personal, family audio recording example because I want to highlight the priceless value of recording and preserving the voices of our family members. A young child changes quickly. Perceptions and ideas of the world change, and voices change. There is great value in recording the voices of people of any age, however, not just young children.

Audio recording can enable you to digitally preserve the voices and memories of people in your own family. It's certainly possible to record family stories with video, but the increased demands of videography can often inhibit the quantity as well as frequency with which we conduct video interviews. Audio-based interviews are less taxing (from a technical perspective) and can be less demanding to conduct. Remember the story of the ceramics teacher shared in the opening chapter, "Why?" **The more media we create and**

archive, the more likely it is we will document compelling stories. Audio recorders can help you record MORE interviews with more people. This process of "playing with media" can help you not only enhance your personal digital literacy skills, but also create compelling media examples because of the larger QUANTITY of media you create.

Storycorps (www.storycorps.org) is a inspiring organization with a wealth of resources on their website to support family as well as community or organizational oral history projects. One of their best resources, related to oral history interviews, is their "Great Questions Generator." [62] You can customize questions for an individual you plan to interview, or download a list of good, open-ended questions which can be used with anyone. Once you "get a taste" of the power and value of digital storytelling, you may want to take your "playing with media" to another level of sophistication and scale.

I hope you will share your media files as well as feedback about your learning journey. There are multiple ways to do this:

1. On Twitter by tweeting with the hashtag #playingwithmedia

2. On Facebook by posting to the wall of the Facebook page for "Playing with Media" [63]

3. On your own blog, by writing a post and then emailing the link to edusandbox@posterous.com. After moderation approval, your post will show up on the blog edusandbox.posterous.com.

---

[62] Great Questions. (n.d.). StoryCorps. Retrieved June 25, 2011, from http://storycorps.org/record-your-story/question-generator/

[63] Fryer, W. (2011). Playing with Media: simple ideas for powerful sharing. Facebook. Retrieved June 24, 2011, from http://www.facebook.com/pages/Playing-with-Media-simple-ideas-for-powerful-sharing/239501402729081

Examples of Classroom Audio Projects

Before exploring different technical options for recording and sharing audio inside and outside the classroom, let's explore some examples of audio recording websites and projects utilized by teachers and students. Audio recording tools are used by learners to improve oral communication skills and fluency. Simply providing students (and older adults) opportunities to hear themselves read aloud can be a powerful and instructive experience. We become more self-aware as oral communicators when we listen to our own voices in audio recordings.[64]

Audio recordings provide a great modality for listening to stories as well as telling stories. While the days of radio-based "fireside chats" are long gone, our students still need to practice LISTENING skills and develop their capacities to focus on a spoken message for a sustained period of time. I'm not suggesting we need to force all children today to listen to two hour sermons sitting in an unpadded, wooden pew like church goers in past generations did, but I AM arguing **the act of focused listening to an audio message is an important skill which can open up numerous doors of learning for students today and in the future.** We live in a mobile society, and in urban areas long commutes are common. Even people living in rural areas often have long bus rides to school and commutes to work. Comfort with and an affinity for listening to spoken audio is useful today given our environment filled with audio podcasts and audiobooks. Helping students learn to both listen to audio recordings and create audio recordings for class assignments

---

[64] Churchhill, P. (2010, November 30). Sound Recording in the Classroom by Paula Churchhill. Moving at the Speed of Creativity. Retrieved June 25, 2011, from http://www.speedofcreativity.org/2010/11/30/sound-recording-in-the-classroom-by-paula-churchhill-cmtc10/

can have instrumental, long-term benefits as well as intrinsic, short-term value.

Read Aloud Audio Projects

One of the most basic ways audio recording tools can be used in the classroom involves students reading their essays aloud into a microphone. This is a good strategy for several reasons. First of all, students do not need to decide what they are going to say when the microphone is turned on and recording: They simply read the essay they have previously written. In addition, read aloud audio projects can be done relatively quickly. Students can rotate through the center or area where recording is done, adding an appropriate title and description to their audio file when finished. While computer software programs like Audacity or handheld digital audio recorders can be used for read aloud projects, web-based audio recording sites and applications which facilitate immediate, online publishing / sharing are simpler to use. The process and workflow for using these different audio recording options in the classroom will be discussed following these examples.

I helped my younger daughter's first grade teacher create her first "read aloud podcast" of student essays. The teacher, Suzie Buxton, had obtained an iPad over Christmas and was interested in using it creatively with students. I suggested we use the free web service and iOS application Cinch, available on Cinch.fm. Each year, Suzie helps her first grade students write "Super Hero Stories." Students work hard on these essays and are very proud of their work when finished. After a short, after-school tutorial session on using the Cinch application on her iPad with me, Suzie had her students rotate through a center in the classroom the next week and record their short Super Hero Stories.[65] Since the Cinch website automatically creates a "table of contents" page for recordings, Suzie was able to email the link to all the parents of children in her class so each one could hear their child reading their essay online.

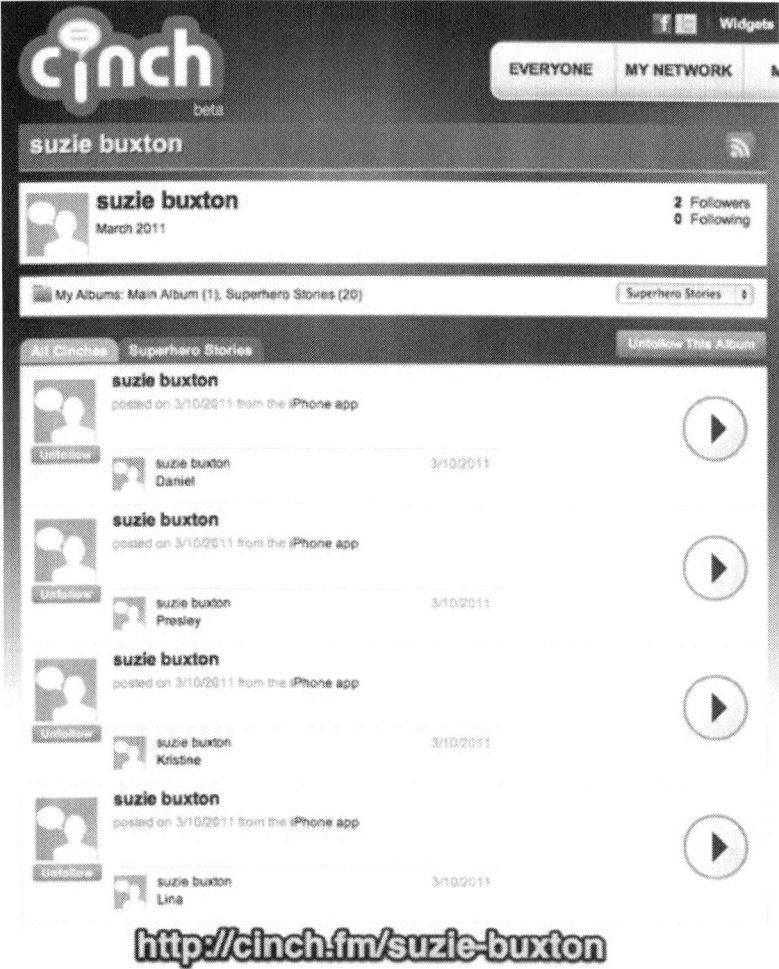

---

[65] Buxton, S. (2011, March 10). Superhero Stories by Suzie Buxton. Cinch.fm. Retrieved June 25, 2011, from http://cinch.fm/suzie-buxton

This was a basic and simple way to use audio in the classroom, but it was also a very exciting and important project. The entire classroom of students was able to record their voices as part of an assignment and share them online for parents and others to enjoy. Given the large amount of time students spend in school, most parents rarely have opportunities to come to school and see what their children are learning. Not only did this read-aloud audio podcasting project provide an opportunity for parents to hear their children read, it also gave the students themselves a chance to hear how they sound as oral readers. Suzie had students label their audio recordings with their first names only, so they and parents could readily identify their own audio recordings.

The streamlined, "minimal click" process involved in this audio project is significant. Had the teacher utilized a hand-held digital audio recorder which requires the transfer of media files from the device to the computer, and from the computer to the Internet, I am certain she and her students would not have been able to complete this project in class the Friday before Spring Break. Since she DID use a "cloud-based" recording and publishing solution like Cinch, however, they did. California educator Marco Torres (alasmedia.wikispaces.com) calls strategies like these "quick victories" for classroom teachers. These are ideas which can be immediately implemented in the classroom with significant, visible benefits. Even if you do not have an iPad or smartphone which can use the free Cinch application, the website permits browser-based recording as well.

Carol Anne McGuire, a California educator known for her digital music sharing project, Rock Our World (www.rockourworld.org), inspired me to create this and other "no edit" podcasting / audio recording projects with students. Several years ago Carol created a simple but powerful "Mothers' Day

Podcast" with students in her classroom.[66] She asked them basic, open ended questions which invited answers which touched the heart. She was teaching primary age students at the time. Some of the questions she asked were:

1. What does your mommy look like?
2. What does your mommy do when you go to school?
3. What do you love about your mom?
4. How does your mom show you she loves you?
5. How do you show your mom you love her?[67]

A couple years later when my younger daughter was in preschool, I worked with her teachers to create a similar podcast with students in her class. I used a battery operated, portable audio recorder and the website gcast.com, which was a free site for phonecasting as well as audio podcast file hosting. The response from teachers and parents for this Mother's Day podcast was, as expected, extremely positive.

One disadvantage of using third-party hosting services for audio podcast sharing (and other media file hosting) is the possibility the site will go out of business and offline. This has happened on two

---

[66] McGuire, C. A. (2007). Podcasts from the VI Room. Rock Our World: The .Mac Website of Carol Anne McGuire. Retrieved June 26, 2011, from http://web.mac.com/rockourworld/iWeb/Site/Podcast/Podcast.html

[67] Fryer, W. (2009, May 3). Bring joy to Mothers in your life this year with a Mother's Day Podcast. Moving at the Speed of Creativity. Retrieved July 23, 2011, from http://www.speedofcreativity.org/2009/05/03/bring-joy-to-mothers-in-your-life-this-year-with-a-mothers-day-podcast/

occasions for me with Mother's Day podcasts. The Mother's Day podcast I created for my wife in 2009 with our children, posted to EduBlogs.tv, is no longer online because EduBlogs discontinued their media hosting service.[68] The Mother's Day podcasts I helped students create in 2009 at my daughter's preschool, which were hosted by the now defunct Gcast.com, are also offline.[69] Problems like these can be averted by downloading local copies of audio podcasts, and/or cross-posting podcasts to more than one website. While some online media losses are inevitable given the dynamic nature of technology companies in the marketplace, these risks can be reduced by utilizing multiple media sites as well as keeping offline copies of favorite work examples.

Field Trip Reflections

As human beings we can remember many more details about an event or experience in our short term memory than our long term memory.[70] Recognizing this neural-cognitive reality, we can and should use audio recording technologies to boost our abilities to document learning experiences like field trips in school. If students

---

[68] Fryer, W. (2009, May 3). Bring joy to Mothers in your life this year with a Mother's Day Podcast. Moving at the Speed of Creativity. Retrieved June 26, 2011, from http://www.speedofcreativity.org/ 2009/05/03/bring-joy-to-mothers-in-your-life-this-year-with-a-mothers-day-podcast/

[69] Fryer, W. (2009). Mother's Day Podcasts 2009 from First Presbyterian Church Preschool, Edmond, Oklahoma. Gcast.com. Verified offline on July 26, 2011, from http://www.gcast.com/u/ wfryer/mothersday2009

[70] Shiffrin, R. M., & Atkinson, R. (1969). Storage and retrieval processes in long-term memory. Psychological Review, 76(2), 179-193.

record thoughts, reflections, and observations during a field trip or immediately following a trip, they can document many more specific details about their experiences. UK educator Joe Dale took his high school students on a field trip to Brittany, France. Each day, a different student recorded a short audio reflection about their experiences and learning that day using the free phonecasting service iPadio.com. On June 29th, students visited Normandy Beach and saw the gravestones of the American soldiers who stormed the beach there in 1945 to liberate Europe from Nazi Germany. Felicity, a student on the trip, recorded a forty-seven second reflection about the day's experiences using a phone and an iPadio account created by Joe Dale.[71]

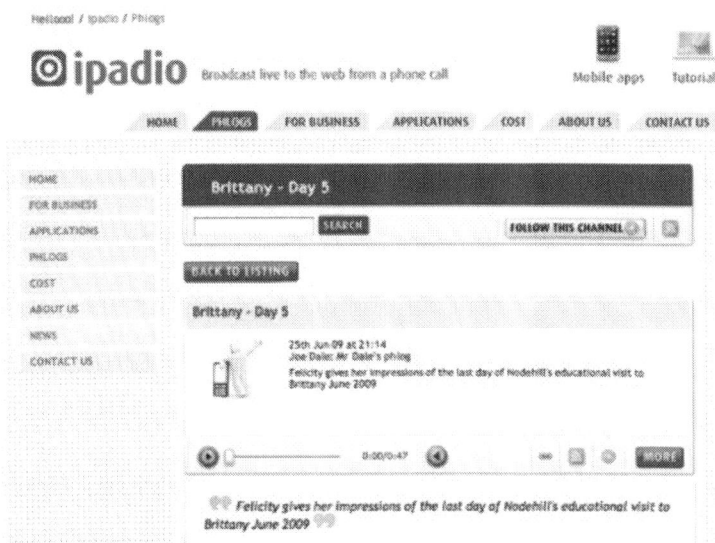

Brittany - Day 5, an iPadio Reflection by Felicity

---

[71] Dale, J. (2009, June 25). Felicity gives her impressions of the last day of Nodehill's educational visit to Brittany June 2009. ipadio | Talk to your World. Retrieved June 25, 2011, from http://www.ipadio.com/phlogs/JoeDale/2009/06/25/Brittany-Day-5

An audio recording like this could be created weeks after the field trip, but there is a qualitative difference when the recording is made "in the moment." You can hear the impact of this visit to the Normandy cemetery in Felicity's tone of voice, as well as the words she shares.

Digital / Electronic Portfolios

Media recordings like this one can and should become part of the "digital portfolio" students amass over the course of their educational careers. When the phrase "electronic portfolio" is mentioned, some people erroneously assume this means schools must pay large sums of money to commercial companies to host and curate electronic materials. While that path is followed by many colleges of education in the United States seeking national accreditation by groups like NCATE, this is not the most appropriate nor cost-effective path for K-12 schools. Although some "digital artifacts" in a student's electronic portfolio could be lost or rendered inaccessible because websites go offline or change terms of service, huge latitude exists for students to create diverse portfolios of work online today. Audio recordings like these can and should become a frequent element in student electronic portfolios.

Some teachers and schools have taken podcasting to the level of professional-quality radio broadcasts, and their work can serve as exemplars for us. Bob Sprankle's third and fourth grade students in Wells, Maine, were featured in an article in the New York Times in 2005 for their podcasting work in Room 208 (bobsprankle.com/

blog).[72] Students and teachers at Willowdale Elementary School in Omaha, Nebraska, regularly author the "Radio WillowWeb" podcast.[73] The use of show segments, audio "bumpers," and shownotes in both the archived Room208 podcasts and the ongoing Radio WillowWeb podcast set a high bar for student podcasters at any level. While more teachers and schools SHOULD emulate these top-bar educational podcasts, we are more likely to see large numbers of learners in schools create and publish shorter, "no edit" or "lightly edited" audio recordings. This latter type of audio media production supports "the ethic of minimal clicks." With fewer steps, more media can be created by more people. These smaller projects don't lessen the importance and value of more polished podcasts, but they do stand out as more practical and "doable" by students in all classrooms.

No-edit audio recordings can be created and shared online in a variety of ways. The two examples I've shared here are just the beginning of a long list of creative ideas for using audio recordings to support learning inside and outside the classroom. Please refer to the "audio" page of the PlayingWithMedia.com website (link at the top of the page, or directly to playingwithmedia.com/pages/audio) for additional ideas.

Online audio files can be created and published using three methods:

---

[72] Todras-Whitehill, E. (2005, August 3). New Tools: Blogs, Podcasts and Virtual Classrooms. The New York Times - Breaking News, World News & Multimedia. Retrieved June 26, 2011, from http://www.nytimes.com/2005/08/03/technology/techspecial3/03ethan.htm

[73] Radio WillowWeb. (n.d.). Willowdale Elementary School - Omaha, Nebraska. Retrieved June 26, 2011, from http://mps.wes.schoolfusion.us/modules/cms/pages.phtml?pageid=115312

1. a cloud-based audio recording service

2. a cloud-based phonecasting service

3. a digital audio recorder

No Edit Audio Recording: Cloud-Based Recorder

Cloud-based audio recording services can simplify the processes of recording, labeling, and sharing audio recordings. Examples of free, cloud-based recording services are AudioBoo.fm, Cinch.fm, and iPadio.com. The diagram below illustrates a three step process for using cloud-based recording services like these.

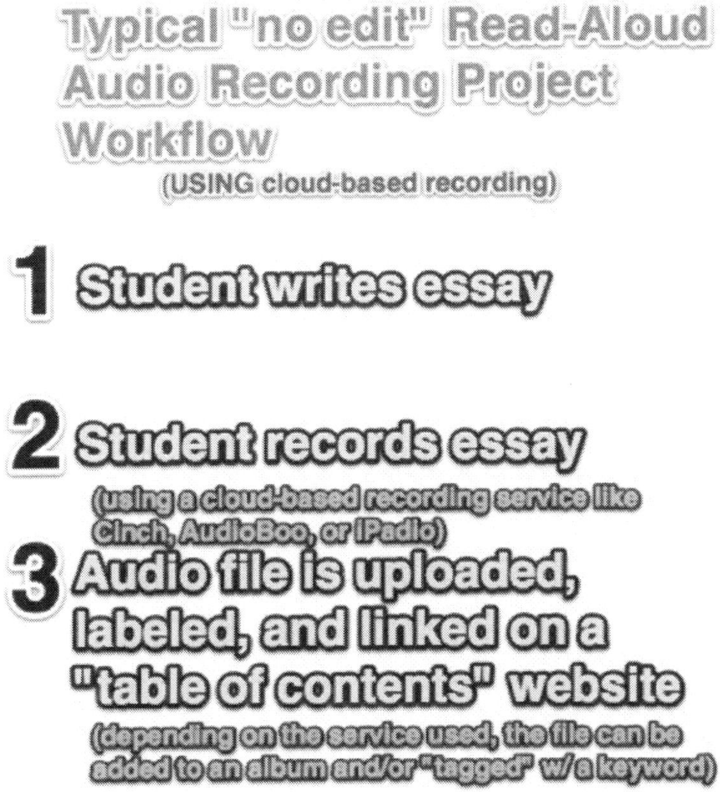

Typical "no edit" Read-Aloud Audio Recording Project Workflow
(USING cloud-based recording)

1 Student writes essay

2 Student records essay
(using a cloud-based recording service like Cinch, AudioBoo, or iPadio)

3 Audio file is uploaded, labeled, and linked on a "table of contents" website
(depending on the service used, the file can be added to an album and/or "tagged" w/ a keyword)

These websites are "cloud-based audio recording" options because they use Internet server software to process information instead of client-side software on your local computer, phone, or other mobile computing device. This is "cloud computing," and as discussed in the "Why" chapter, it opens up myriad possibilities for digital sharers like us.

Most cloud-based audio recording sites not only permit browser-based recording, using a microphone connected to your computer, but also support smartphone app / application recording and publishing. Both AudioBoo and iPadio have free apps for iOS and Android phones. Cinch has an iOS app.

AudioBoo

Here are the specific steps for using the website AudioBoo.fm to create a no-edit audio podcast episode.

1. **Connect a microphone** to your computer or plan to use the built-in microphone, if available. Test the microphone in the control panels / system preferences to verify it is selected as the recording device and is working.

2. **Log in to AudioBoo.com** with your account, which you'll want to create and test in advance of your student lesson. If you are working with older students (over 13) they can create their own accounts, but their recordings will NOT be in the same channel or "table of contents" site if they use them. It's easier from a management standpoint to have students use an account you create for class use. I strongly recommend NOT providing students with the account credentials (userid and password) for the

account, but instead log into the site yourself and allow students to use it in class on an available computer.

3. **Click MY PROFILE** in AudioBoo and then the red, RECORD button in your web browser.

4. **Click NEW RECORDING** in the left side of the popup window which should appear in your web browser. If you don't see the popup window, change your browser settings to permit popups from AudioBoo.fm. (If you run into trouble with this step concerning popups, ask a young person to help you figure this out!)

5. **Approve the Java-plugin** message when prompted. If prompted to approve an Applet from AudioBoo, also click approve.

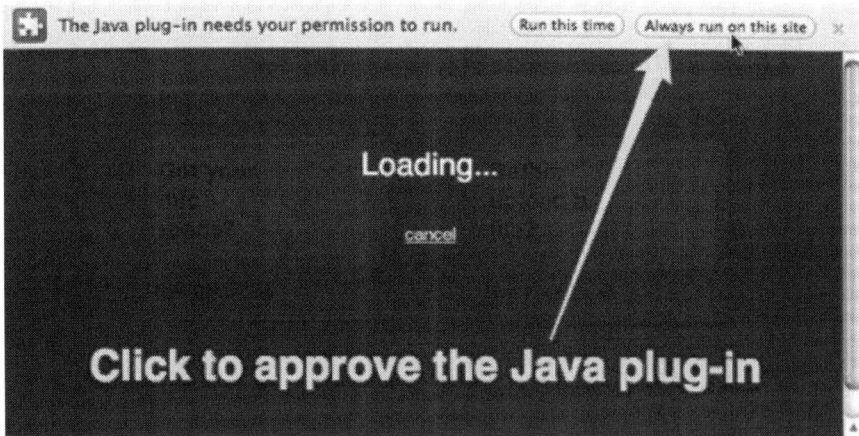

6. **Click START RECORDING** and record your audio message, up to five minutes in length.

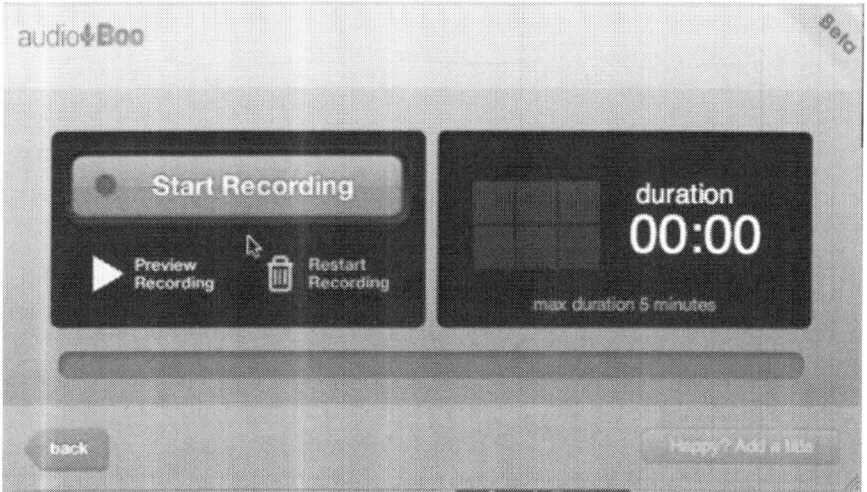

If desired, you can pause the recording and play back what you've made so far. You can also restart the recording and try again.

Note that creating a "no edit" audio recording or podcast does not mean "record your first try and accept it with all the mistakes you make." In fact, what you'll often find as students start to use audio recording sites like AudioBoo is a pattern: Many students will iteratively record and listen to themselves, trying again till they get it right. In some cases you might consider setting a limit for the number of "re-dos" students have for their recording, since time is likely limited for you in class. From technological and financial perspectives, however, there is no reason students can't try making their recording as many times as they want.

7. **Add a title to your AudioBoo** when you are satisfied with your recording, by clicking the green "Happy? Add a title" button in the lower right corner of the recording popup window. You can add three different kinds of information to your AudioBoo: Info (including a title and tags, which are like keywords used later for finding your recording), an image, and a map location. Everyone should add a title and tags, but the image and map location are optional.

Consider using a unique "tag" just for your class, so you can search for that tag on the AudioBoo site later and quickly locate all the recordings created by your students. Using a unique, common tag is a way students can use their own AudioBoo accounts but the media they create can still be findable / digitally aggregateable on the site. (Aggregation is the process of filtering content and gathering just the items you want.)

Before sharing an image of a student in an AudioBoo, be sure both the student and parent have granted permission for online photo publication by signing your school or district's media sharing form. Often it is NOT necessary or desirable to share a photo of the student in an AudioBoo: Instead a photograph of some accompanying art they created or something else relating to the topic of the "Boo" can be attached. Creative Commons licensed images, discussed in an upcoming chapter, can be great to include here.

Take care when sharing a location in an AudioBoo, especially if you are creating audio recordings at your home. It's probably fine to add location information when you're on a field trip or at school, but the privacy concerns this raises for home addresses should be avoided. Talk to your students about what it means to "geo-tag media" (add a specific map location which others can use to find where that file was created.) Geo-tagging is powerful and can be used in very constructive ways, but it also can raise real privacy issues when sharing media from home. The global AudioBoo map (audioboo.fm/boos/map) shows the locations of AudioBoos in many different locations. Try zooming in to view Boos created by people in your area of the planet.

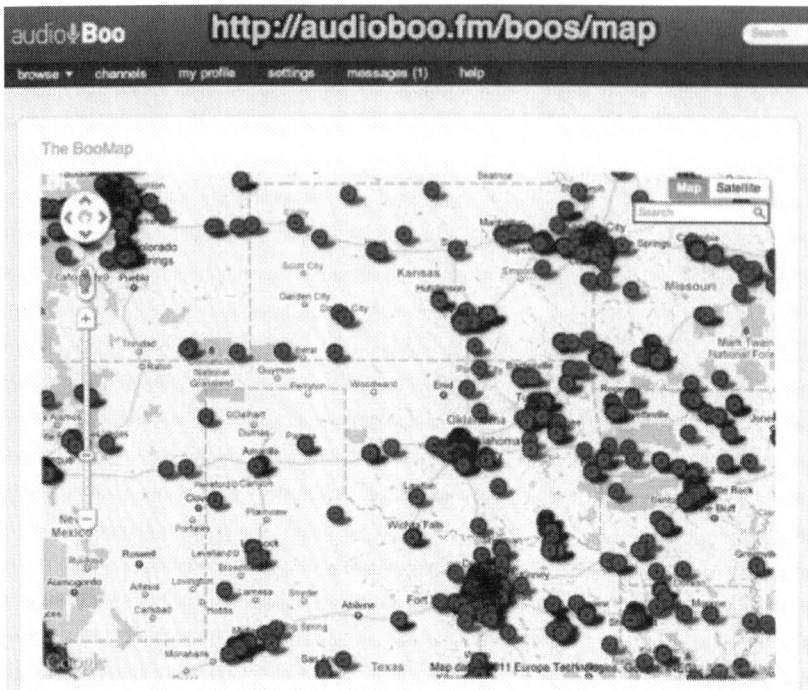

The screenshot shows a browser window with the URL http://audioboo.fm/boos/map and navigation tabs, displaying "The BooMap" with map markers across a region of the United States.

The Boo Map by AudioBoo [74]

By default, all AudioBoo.fm and Cinch.fm recordings are PUBLIC and viewable by anyone in the world with the link to the recording. AudioBoos and Cinches are listed on the public / main AudioBoo and Cinch websites, so people can "browse" to your recordings without you linking to them on your class website or emailing the link to them. iPadio.com (described in detail next) is the only site of these three which permits users to designate recordings as PRIVATE rather than public. In the case of private recordings on iPadio, however, ONLY the person logged into the iPadio website is able to view those files.

---

[74] The BooMap. (n.d.). Audioboo. Retrieved July 24, 2011, from http://audioboo.fm/boos/map

When creating cloud-based, no-edit audio recordings with students, it's best to create them for public sharing. This means any privacy and confidentiality rules for media sharing in your school or district should be followed.

No Edit Audio Recording: Phonecasting

Phonecasting is a process involving use of a telephone to record an audio message subsequently shared publicly on the World Wide Web. The word "phonecast" is a portmanteau of the words phone and podcasting. Since many students in schools today have their own cell phones, phonecasting services offer an attractive option for creating and sharing no-edit audio recordings or podcasts.

Commercial companies offering phonecasting services have come and gone, but the potential to use telephones to record and share audio files online is a persistent or transcendent capability. Even if one or more of the companies mentioned here closes its doors in the years ahead, I'm confident others will emerge. Phones are ubiquitous in the developed world, and the ways in which phonecasts can be used constructively to support learning are only starting to be realized.

An updated list of phonecasting services is available on the PlayingWithMedia Audio page (playingwithmedia.com/pages/audio.) Of those listed, two I recommend are iPadio.com and Cinch.fm. The diagram below shows the feature differences between iPadio, Cinch and AudioBoo.

Feature Comparison: No-Edit Cloud-Based Audio Recording

	ⓘ ipadio	cinch	audio Boo
Phonecasting	Yes	Yes	No
Browser-based recording	No	Yes	Yes
iOS App	Yes	Yes	Yes
Android App	Yes	Yes	Yes
Accepts Uploads	Yes	No	Yes
Free?	Yes	Yes	Yes

Created by Wesley Fryer 8/28/2011

More Info on PlayingWithMedia.com

To create a phonecast with either iPadio or Cinch:

1. **Register for a free account** on iPadio.com and/or Cinch.fm. Alternatively, download the free smartphone applications for iOS or Android on their respective websites and register via the app.

2. **Call the phonecasting number** for the service you are using. It's best to use a cell phone to phonecast, since cell phone "minutes" are used but long distance changes don't apply. Neither iPadio nor Cinch currently have maximum time limits for recorded phonecasts. Cinch uses a single, global phone number: (646) 200-0000. In your account profile for Cinch, you need to identify phones which will be associated with your account and directly publish to your channel. These can be connected directly to specific albums, so you can (if desired) enter your students' phone numbers and "map" their Cinch phonecasts to post directly to their personal album in your Cinch account. iPadio, on the other hand, uses different phone numbers based on the country where you live.[75] The iPadio phone number for the United States is (866) 488-3946.

3. **Check your phonecast channel site** several minutes after hanging up your phone call to test the web-posted version of your audio recording. If desired, copy the link and/or "embed code" for a specific episode and email it to parents or post it to a blog or wiki site.

---

[75] iPadio International Phone Numbers. (n.d.). iPadio | Talk to your World. Phonecast live to the web from any phone, anywhere. Retrieved June 26, 2011, from http://ipadio.com/page.asp? section=79&sectionTitle=ipadio+international+phone+numbers

If you want to enable students to directly <u>phonecast</u> to a channel you've created, Cinch is a better choice than iPadio. You can add student cell phone numbers directly to your Cinch account, and even assign separate channels for their phonecasts. After logging into Cinch.fm, click the SETTINGS button under your account icon and select PHONE options.

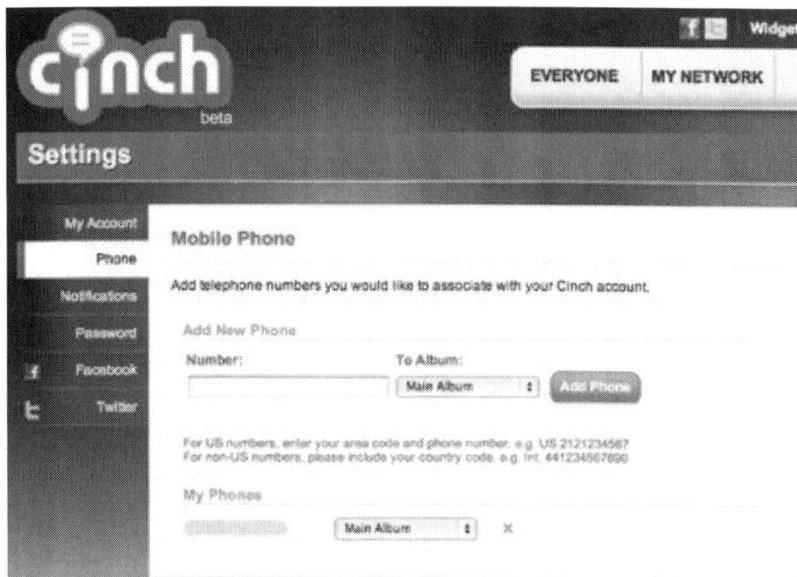

iPadio limits accounts to only two authorized phone numbers for direct phonecasting. You could provide students with your cell phone number and iPadio channel PIN, but this is NOT recommended. This is equivalent to providing them with your username and password for your entire iPadio channel. It is never a good idea to provide students with your personal login credentials for a website account.

Be aware content moderation is NOT currently available for phonecasts on either iPadio or Cinch.fm. If students are over 13 and using iPadio, consider having them phonecast to their own channels / accounts and then sharing links to their phonecasts via your moderated class blog. As described above, Cinch can be used for phonecasts if you enter their authorized phone numbers into your account settings.

In the past I have created phonecasts as final examination reviews for students in pre-service teacher education classes.[76] This idea came from Eric Langhorst (ericlanghorst.com), an 8th grade US History teacher in Liberty, Missouri, and the 2007-2008 Missouri Teacher of the Year. Eric's "Speaking of History" podcast (speakingofhistory.blogspot.com) is an exemplary classroom teacher "media channel."

When you are logged into your iPadio or Cinch account, individual episodes have both direct links and "embed code" which can be used to put a snazzy player button on another website which can be used to play your phonecast. The image below shows where these links appear on an iPadio episode, when logged into your account. Note with iPadio, channel owners can also download phonecast episodes as MP3 files. This is handy if you or a student wants to combine phonecasts and create an aggregated version of several recordings.

[76] Fryer, W. (2011, April 29). Final Exam Study Guide - Technology 4 Teachers. iPadio | Talk to your World. Phonecast live to the web from any phone, anywhere | ipadio | Talk to your World. Retrieved June 26, 2011, from http://www.ipadio.com/phlogs/WesleyFryer/2011/4/29/Final-Exam-Study-Guide--Technology-4-Teachers

ipadio Broadcast live to the web from a phone call

HOME | PHLOGS | FOR BUSINESS | APPLICATIONS | COST | ABOUT US | CONTACT US

HOME
FOR BUSINESS
APPLICATIONS
PHLOGS
COST
ABOUT US
NEWS
CONTACT US

Final Exam Study Guide - Technology 4 Teachers

SEARCH   FOLLOW THIS CHANNEL

BACK TO LISTING

Final Exam Study Guide - Technology 4 Teachers

29th Apr 11 at 04:36
Wesley Fryer: Wesley's phlog
This twelve minute audio recording is a study guide for students enrolled in Technology 4 Teachers at the University of Central Oklahoma in Spring 2011, in sections taught by Wesley Fryer.

DOWNLOAD
EDIT
DELETE

Short URL: http://ipad.io/aKF Tags: t4t, technology, edtech
Lake Hefner Pkwy, Oklahoma City, OK 73120, USA

0:07/11:48   MORE

Episode shortened link

<object classid="clsid:d27cdb6e-ae6d-11cf-96b8-444...   ...000" codebase="http://download.mac

Stats

This twelve minute audio recording is a study guide for students enrolled in Technology 4 Teachers at the University of Central Oklahoma in Spring 2011, in sections taught by Wesley Fryer.

Get episode embed code

Three-Party Phonecasting (for interviews)

Free phonecasting services like iPadio.com can not only be used to record your voice or record the voices of your students who call in to your "channel," they also can be used to record phone interviews conducted with more than one person. A five minute screencast

104

demonstrating this process with iPadio and a phone which supports three-way calling is available on YouTube.[77]

No Edit Audio Recording: Digital Audio Recorder

Every classroom should ideally have at least one battery operated digital audio recorder for student use, and school libraries should have digital audio recorders available for student and teacher checkout. Battery operated digital audio recorders can be plugged directly into a computer via USB, do not require recharging, can typically record hundreds of hours of audio, and do not require removable micro-cassettes: They store data with onboard flash memory. This photo shows older Olympus WS-110 digital audio recorders used in the initial years of the Celebrate Oklahoma Voices oral history project (lc.celebrateoklahoma.us).[78]

---

[77] How to record a phone interview as a phonecast using iPadio.com. (n.d.). Screenr | Instant screencasts: Just click record. Retrieved June 2, 2011, from http://www.screenr.com/rA5. Also available on www.youtube.com/watch?v=Ds5jTOgD_JY

[78] Fryer, W. (2007, January 7). Olympus WS-110 Recorders. Flickr - Photo Sharing. Retrieved June 26, 2011, from http://www.flickr.com/photos/wfryer/3199766045/in/set-72157612571742431/

A variety of digital audio recorders are available on the market with widely varying prices. Good quality, digital recorders are available in the United States from $25 to $60. It is certainly possible to spend more than $100 on a digital audio recorder, but an expensive model is not required for classroom use. Storychasers maintains current, linked lists of equipment included in the "digital backpack" of digital storytelling equipment participants receive as supplies during the "phase 1" two day workshop for teachers (storychasers.org/faq/#Digital+Backpack+Contents). WalMart currently sells an RCA model which is USB-ready (it doesn't require a cable, the USB port extends out "switchblade style") for $25.[79] This kind of recorder can work well in the classroom.

---

[79] RCA VR5320 1GB Digital Voice Recorder. (n.d.). WalMart.com. Retrieved July 26, 2011, from http://www.walmart.com/ip/RCA-VR5320-1GB-Digital-Voice-Recorder/15183948

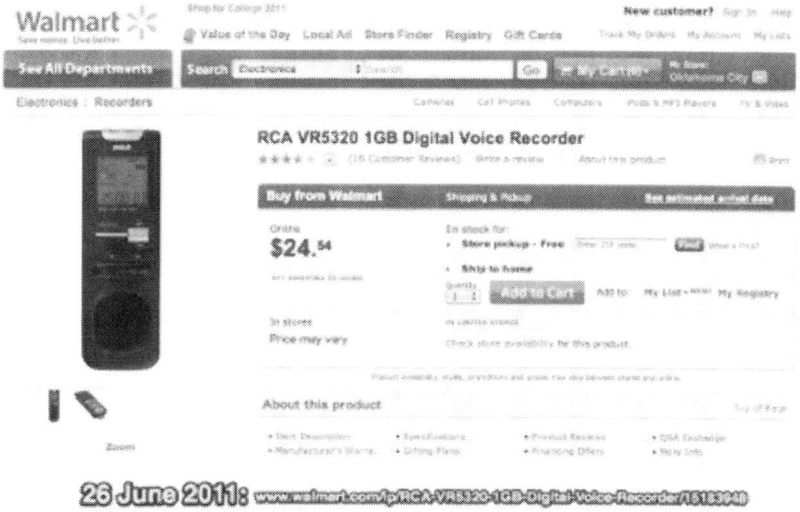

RCA Digital Voice Recorder on Walmart.com in June 2011

The following graphic illustrates the main steps involved in creating a "no edit" digital audio recording project with a portable audio recorder.

Typical "no edit" Read-Aloud Audio Recording Project Workflow

(NOT using cloud-based recording, using digital audio recorder)

1 Student writes essay

2 Student records essay
(using a digital audio recorder)

3 Audio file is transferred from the digital audio recorder to a computer
(appropriate file name is used, correct file location is used for saving)

4 Audio file is uploaded online

5 Audio file is linked from a "table of contents" website

No-edit Read Aloud Audio Recording: With Digital Audio Recorder
by Wesley Fryer [80]

---

[80] Fryer, W. (2011, June 25). No-edit Read Aloud Audio Recording: With Digital Audio Recorder. Flickr - Photo Sharing. Retrieved July 23, 2011, from http://www.flickr.com/photos/wfryer/5869872306/

In projects like this, I recommend using a website specifically formatted for audio uploads and browser-based audio playback. The websites iPadio.com and AudioBoo.fm both support audio uploads. iPadio requires audio files be in mp3 format for uploading, but AudioBoo accepts most audio formats including mp3, WAV, and AIFF.

The previous sentence included several technical file types which really do NOT have to be part of conversations when creating audio recordings for a school project. If you use a digital audio recorder for your project, however, it's possible you will need to learn about file formats and conversion tools. Remember "the ethic of minimal clicks," discussed previously? This is an example of why cloud-based audio recording and sharing websites are preferable to digital audio recorders in many cases. Even though digital audio recorders are truly "wireless" (except when transferring files to a computer) and are relatively less expensive than video recorders, they require "more steps" for publishing than tools like AudioBoo. WikiPedia is a good resource for definitions of audio file formats.[81]

Note the previous workflow diagram for a digital audio recorder "no edit" podcast has five steps. Removing several of these steps can be a WONDERFUL thing and make these kinds of projects much more practical in the classroom. If you are going to use a digital audio recorder, however, here are some suggestions for steps 3 - 5 which may help you and your students. Remember **STEP 1** is when students write their essay, and **STEP 2** is when they record their essay with an audio recorder. A microphone connected to a computer can be used with free software like Audacity (audacity.sourceforge.net) but I've found the relative simplicity of digital audio recorders (they have fewer options to select than

---

[81] Audio file format. (n.d.). Wikipedia, the free encyclopedia. Retrieved July 4, 2011, from http://en.wikipedia.org/wiki/Audio_file_format#List_of_formats

software programs) make them work better with students in the classroom for recording.

STEP 3: Audio File is Transferred from the Digital Audio Recorder to a Computer

Digital audio recorders like the RCA model shown previously have several internal folders for recording audio. Alert your students to this fact and at a minimum, ask them to write down which folder they used when recording their audio. You might assign them a folder on the recorder to use. If you have a classroom of 20 or more students, it can be complicated to sort out whose files are in which folder of the recorder, especially if students don't write down the folder they've used. Most digital audio recorders have five folders, either named A - E or 1 through 5.

When digital audio files are transferred to the computer, be sure the person making the transfers gives each file a logical name which makes sense. It is good to use the last name of the person who made the recording. This process can be time consuming and complicated. Consider having a student do this for you. When your students are recording, have them write down their name on a list which goes with the recorder, identifying which file numbers in which folders they recorded. This list can be an invaluable index for you and your students to use when trying to figure out who recorded each separate file.

When transferring audio files to the computer, in addition to naming the files appropriately make sure you create and use appropriate folders or directories on the computer. You might use different folders for each class, or for each project group in the class. Organizing from the start is generally the best idea. If you have a lot of audio files all saved in the same folder on your computer, it can be difficult to make sense of them.

Consider using a standard file naming syntax for audio files. It helps to use the date and start with the year. A format could be: year-month-day-lastname. An example file named with this syntax woud be 2011-06-26-fryer. Remember not to use special characters in your filenames. It is also good to avoid spaces in file names, especially if you'll be uploading the files to the Internet.

One of the biggest benefits of using a portable digital audio recorder is also a drawback: Live Internet access is NOT required for recording. While the cloud-based audio recording methods described previously can streamline these steps, they also require good bandwidth / connectivity to complete. If your school or location does NOT have a good Internet connection speed, specifically when your students are in class and will be making audio recordings, consider using a portable digital audio recorder instead of a website. It can save lots of bandwidth headaches since files can be shared / uploaded later.

If all this sounds a bit complicated, that's because IT IS... relatively speaking.

As described in the previous section, using a cloud-based audio recording solution can ELIMINATE steps (thereby supporting "the ethic of minimal clicks") and make this process simpler and faster for both you and your students.

Closing Thoughts

I hope the ideas in this chapter have encouraged you to not only become a more avid consumer of audio content via free podcasts, but also a content CREATOR with audio. There are several other audio recording / podcasting related resources I want to commend to you.

EdTechTalk (edtechtalk.com) is an open, collaborative community of educational webcasters. Webcasting, in contrast to podcasting, is a "live" activity happening synchronously over the Internet. In addition to broadcasting (or "narrowcasting," depending on your terminology preferences) webcasts EdTechTalk also publishes recorded versions of webcasts as podcasts. As podcasts, these files can be downloaded and consumed at the time and location of your preference. I highly commend EdTechTalk to you and their wonderful selection of shows. Everything on EdTechTalk is free. Seedlings (edtechtalk.com/seedlings,) a production of Bob Sprankle, Cheryl Oakes and Alice Barr, is one of my favorite regular shows. I have learned an enormous amount over the years from Bob, Cheryl, Alice and their webshow guests. The fact that they live in Maine and I live in Oklahoma is not an impediment to my ability to learn from them on a regular basis. Such is the nature of blended learning, powered by media sharing, in the 21st century.[82] It is a wonderful blessing to be able to learn alongside passionate educators and geeks like "The Seedlings." Their keynote for the K-12 Online Conference, "How Can I Become Part of this ReadWriteWeb Revolution?" is an excellent, twenty-five minute video presentation well worth your time to check out.[83]

EdReach, the Education Media Network (edreach.us) is another audio podcasting resource I want to spotlight and commend to you. The EdReach vision is to provide:

---

[82] Fryer, W. (2011, April 2). Cheryl Oakes, Wesley Fryer, Alice Barr, Sarah Fryer, and Bob Sprankle. Flickr - Photo Sharing. Retrieved June 26, 2011, from http://www.flickr.com/photos/wfryer/4487424301/

[83] Sprankle, B., Oakes, C., & Barr, A. (2008, October 28). GETTING STARTED KEYNOTE "How Can I Become Part of this ReadWriteWeb Revolution?" K-12 Online Conference. Retrieved July 22, 2011, from http://k12onlineconference.org/?p=269

a platform for passionate, outspoken educators- aiming to strengthen their voices by highlighting innovation in the field of education, through reporting critical educational news and providing commentary and criticism of the educational issues of the day.[84]

As we continue to experience media convergence in the months and years ahead, non-traditional media outlets like EdReach can and will play an increasingly important role in the ways we learn about and share news. I am not affiliated with EdReach, but I concur with the goals and vision of its founders and commend it to you as a great resource.

Although it is not an organization focused on publishing podcasts, I would be remiss if I did not mention and commend the **Classroom 2.0 Network** (www.classroom20.com) in this list. Not only is Classroom 2.0 the largest online network of educators in a Ning network (over 57,000 at this writing) it's also a wonderful place to participate in live as well as recorded events touching on a variety of technology integration issues. The Classroom 2.0 Live site (live.classroom20.com) has a packed calendar of free learning events year-round.

Finally, I want to share encouragement for you to check out and participate in the annual **K-12 Online Conference** (www.k12onlineconference.org). Since 2006, K12Online has published over forty high quality video presentations by educators around the world about technology integration and new tools for both teaching and learning. The K-12 Online Conference is entirely FREE. There are (at this writing) over two hundred free video and audio presentations in podcast-downloadable formats. Visit the

---

[84] About | EdReach. (n.d.). EdReach- The Education Media Network. Retrieved June 26, 2011, from http://edreach.us/about/

conference website page for web feeds for more information and subscription links.[85]

You can be a key part of the "solution" we need in our classrooms and schools today to usher in a revolution in the ways we learn. I challenge you to play with some of the audio tools and strategies highlighted in this chapter, and facilitate a lesson with your students in the upcoming year which makes use of "no-edit" audio recordings. When you do, I hope you'll share your learning with others via the "Playing with Media" Facebook page, Twitter hashtag (#playingwithmedia) and your own blog.

When we share our learning, we can all get better.

Read Appendix C: Audio Software & Lecturecasts for more information about podcatchers (software used for podcast subscriptions,) audio creation and conversion tools. Free software options for audio lecturecasting is also addressed.

---

[85] K-12 Online Conference Web feeds. (n.d.). K12 Online Conference. Retrieved June 26, 2011, from http://k12onlineconference.org/?page_id=147

4- Copyright & Fair Use

Creative Commons Logo [86]

(Because of the importance and relevance of this information to ALL learners playing with media, an updated version of this chapter is available on playingwithmedia.com/pages/copyright.)

Copyright, fair use, and intellectual property issues are important for students, educators, and other citizens. As digital learners not only "consuming" media but also CREATING and SHARING

---

[86] Czerepak, G. (2009, March 18). Creative Commons: Proposed Protection Categories. relationary.wordpress. Retrieved June 27, 2011, from http://soliver8.wordpress.com/2011/06/06/week-10-why-i-chose-my-creative-commons-licence/

media, we need simple and accurate guidelines to follow as we are "playing with media." The guidelines below are designed primarily for people in the United States, but may apply to other locations. Please read my disclaimer in this endnote.[87] You may want to use the following mnemonic to remember copyright and fair use guidelines relating to media sharing and fair use.

Harry Potter Can Fly

- H = Homegrown
- P = Public Domain
- C = Creative Commons
- F = Fair Use

"Harry Potter Can Fly" by Rachel Fryer [88]

---

[87] Legal disclaimer on Copyright / Intellectual Property Issues: The author of these guidelines, Wesley Fryer, is not a lawyer and the information included on this website and book project should not be interpreted as official, legal advice. Copyright laws vary by country. For legal advice about intellectual property issues in the jurisdiction where you live pertaining to specific copyright situations, consult a bar-certified lawyer in your area.

[88] Fryer, R. (2011, June 4). Harry Potter Can Fly! by Rachel Fryer. Flickr - Photo Sharing. Retrieved July 4, 2011, from http://www.flickr.com/photos/wfryer/5798145636/in/set-72157626886284140/

Homegrown

Media you create yourself is "homegrown." Pictures in an old shoebox in your grandmother's attic, which she gives you permission to photograph or scan and share on the Internet, are an example of homegrown media. You own the copyright to homegrown media, so you decide how to use it digitally. Generally you should obtain permission from people whose photographs you take and use online. You cannot take photographs of copyrighted or trademarked icons (like Disney's Mickey Mouse logo) and use them for any purpose, like a commercial product. There ARE some limits to homegrown media uses.

Public Domain

Public domain works are shared by everyone. Some types of works are explicitly published in the public domain (like photographs by NASA) while others "pass into the public domain" after their period of copyright protection expires. As the Digital Copyright Slider illustrates, it can be challenging to determine if certain works remain protected by copyright or are in the public domain. Websites like WikiPedia generally provide explicit information about the copyright status of included works, like photographs, noting if a work is believed to be in the public domain. Public domain works can be used for commercial or non-commercial purposes without getting anyone's permission, and are NOT subject to "fair use" provisions of U.S. copyright law. Their potential use and re-use is unrestricted.

Creative Commons

Creative Commons licensed-media are shared "up front" by copyright holders for sharing and re-use under certain terms. This means "permission has already been granted" for you to use these media materials in your own projects, as long as you comply with the stated Creative Commons terms. Creative Commons provides free licenses to anyone publishing media. For example, the "Playing with Media" eBook is licensed under Creative Commons. Millions of Creative Commons licensed images, audio files, and video files are now available. By using Creative Commons licensed media in your projects (giving proper attribution to the author/owner) you can comply with US copyright law AND support a growing culture of online collaboration. You can also support the culture of legal, online sharing by licensing YOUR shared works online under Creative Commons. Learn more by watching Creative Commons videos. (creativecommons.org/videos)

Fair Use

Fair use provisions are included in U.S. Copyright law. These parts of our legal code provide guidelines and criteria for determining when specific uses of copyrighted works ARE permissible and legal WITHOUT granted permission from the author / owner. Fair use is NOT a right, it is a legal defense in the event someone is accused of copyright infringement. The law does NOT provide "bright line" rules for determining fair use. This was attempted by the 1986 Fair Use Guidelines for Educational Media, but those guidelines are NOT the law and should not be construed as such because in some cases they are unnecessarily and overly restrictive. The short video chapter on "Fair Use" (1 min, 50 sec) included in Professor Eric Faden of Bucknell University's video "A Fair(y) Use Tale" illustrates key concepts of fair use in U.S. copyright law exclusively using short clips from copyrighted Disney movies. The full video is 10 minutes, 14 seconds long.

Learning About Attribution with WikiPedia

One of the many virtues of WikiPedia is the explicit copyright and usage rights information which its authors and editors post with photos. The following copyright information accompanies the famous "Blue Marble" photograph taken by NASA astronauts on the Apollo 17 mission in 1972.

Blue Marble [89]

As a classroom teacher discussing copyright and <u>fair use</u> with your students, utilize WikiPedia images to discuss usage rights and published terms for reusing media files. NASA images are some of the best to utilize to show examples of <u>public domain</u> images.

---

[89] The Earth seen from Apollo 17.jpg. (1972, December 7). Wikipedia, the free encyclopedia. Retrieved June 4, 2011, from <u>http://en.wikipedia.org/wiki/</u> <u>File:The_Earth_seen_from_Apollo_17.jpg</u>

Summary

Anyone who tells you copyright and fair use issues are simple in the United States is either naive, poorly informed, or both. Intellectual property law IS complicated, and conversations about copyright issues tend to leave participants more confused rather than clear about guidelines. Because of this reality, I have tried to make this chapter as brief and concise as possible. Most people "playing with media" do not want to take a semester course or get a degree on copyright, they simply need clear guidelines.

Attribution, in the form of a thorough "Works Cited" section of a document or project, does NOT guarantee full copyright compliance in the United States. Judges ruling on intellectual property cases never write, "The defendant created a great bibliography, so I find find him not guilty of these charges." Properly attributing sources in writing and media projects is an important part of "how we work" as academics and scholars. Attribution is also an important part of Creative Commons license compliance. As teachers and leaders, we need to model attribution "best practices" for our students and encourage them to do the same.

Attribution of sources should be specific, not general. Frequently in school media projects around the United States, however, teachers accept student work which either lacks attribution or lacks attribution specificity. We would never accept the following entry in a written, student bibliography in a research paper:

I found this information in the school library.

We should not accept student media projects which include similar, non-specific attribution statements like "Images from Google" or "Images from Flickr." **Attribution takes time, but it is an important part of what we do as ethical writers, researchers, and media communicators**. Utilize free, online resources to streamline the attribution process.

I used the free website service Bibme.org to create the attribution citations for this book. BibMe is web-based and permits users to create separate bibliographies accessible from any Internet-connected computer web browser. Entries can be formatted in MLA, APA, or other formats with the click of a mouse. Remember "the ethic of minimal clicks?" Cloud-based services like BibMe support this ethic. Other outstanding attribution sites and tools are available and should be used by your students.

This chapter is intended to be a practical guide for students, teachers, librarians, school administrators, and others creating and sharing media online. In the United States, we have generous fair use laws and need to exercise our rights of free expression. The Media and Education Lab at Temple University has an outstanding collection of resources on Copyright and Fair Use, which also encourage the EXERCISE of free speech rights in digital spaces by students as well as educators. In addition to those resources, check the copyright links provided on the Playing with Media website (playingwithmedia.com/pages/copyright.)

5- Images

Images by Rachel Fryer [90]

Images are powerful. We and our students need to understand the potential for images to influence our ideas and behavior, as we see in product marketing. We also need to practice the use of images as effective multimedia communicators.

When I was initially brainstorming ideas for this book, I considered the title, "Talking with Media." I even registered the domain talkwithmedia.com, but eventually decided "Playing with Media" would be a better title. Images "talk to us" all the time,

---

[90] Fryer, R. (2011, July 1). Images by Rachel Fryer. Flickr - Photo Sharing. Retrieved July 2, 2011, from http://www.flickr.com/photos/wfryer/5891685063/in/set-72157626886284140/

sometimes in ways we do not fully acknowledge or understand. How many logos and brands can a toddler who has not yet started school recognize? Corporations like McDonalds and Disney understand and leverage the power of images constantly in their corporate marketing and branding campaigns. As Naomi Klein highlighted in her eye opening book, No Logo, parents, educators, and policymakers need to be aware of the strategic and intentional ways corporations build and maintain brand loyalty from a very young age utilizing media marketing.[91] We need to help students develop greater senses and skills of media literacy as consumers and citizens in our digital age. As I argued in the introductory chapter, the most effective and powerful way to help students develop their media literacy skills is by helping them become MEDIA PRODUCERS in addition to more savvy MEDIA CONSUMERS.

As we are playing with media and seeking ways to more effectively "talk with media" inside and outside the classroom, we need to practice strategies for effectively finding and using images created by others. In addition, we need skills and tools for creating and remixing our own images, while complying with the intellectual property laws of our nation. In this chapter, I'll address both these needs.

Copyright Friendly Image Sources

While many students as well as teachers frequently use Google Images (images.google.com) to find photos to use in multimedia projects, many other Internet websites are available which are preferable as image sources. In many classrooms around the United States today, Google Images is the most-frequently used website for image use in classroom projects which neither respect intellectual

---

[91] Klein, N. (2001). No logo. London: Flamingo.
www.naomiklein.org/no-logo

property law (regarding fair use) or attempt to properly attribute image ownership. [92] This trend needs to change, and that process begins with each one of us as teachers as we help students in their multimedia projects.

Reasons to use alternate websites (other than Google Images) for project photos include:

1. **Who really owns an image?** Ownership for Internet images indexed by Google can be difficult or impossible to determine. Who actually owns the image and should be credited for it?

2. **Licensed usage rights**: What are the copyright owners' terms for reusing the image without permission? Most students as well as teachers utilize "simple keyword" Google Image searches, rather than advanced searches filtered by license. Most images indexed by Google today do NOT clearly specify sharing rights.

3. **Surprising and Objectionable image search results**: Although "SafeSearch" options to "Use moderate filtering" and "Use strict filtering" on Google Images definitely improves the relevance as well as propriety of many image search results, it is still relatively easy to be surprised by the results of Google Image keyword searches. At worst, students can be subjected to offensive, inappropriate images using a Google Image search for seemingly innocuous word phrases.

---

[92] In the summer of 2010, Google added new options in its "advanced image search" menu, permitting "filtering by license" or "usage rights." Although this is a welcome improvement to Google Image searches for learners wanting to comply with copyright law as well as correctly attribute image sources, it is generally NOT advisable to use Google Images as your primary source of visual media to reuse and repurpose. Usage rights : Features - Web Search Help. (n.d.). Google. Retrieved June 4, 2011, from http://www.google.com/support/websearch/bin/answer.py?&answer=29508

It is NEVER a good idea to perform a "live image search" in front of a classroom or group of students on the Google Images site, or on almost any other image web search engine site. Even if you've tried an image search on a specific site previously, there are no guarantees what the new results of a dynamic image search may be today. With these ideas in mind, it is good to explore other image search options in addition to Google Images. It's also a good idea to practice image search demonstrations you want to share with students in advance, to prevent an "embarrassing Internet image moment" in front of your class.

Please do not misunderstand me: I'm a BIG fan of almost "anything Google" and DO use Google Images myself at times. This includes contexts in which I'm working with younger students as well as adult educators. Google Images is NOT my first recommended source for Internet image searches, however, and I encourage you to move it "down your list" of sites to utilize as well for the reasons I've outlined.

As discussed in the preceding chapter on Copyright and Fair Use, it's always a good idea to consider HOMEGROWN and PUBLIC DOMAIN image sources before searching for copyrighted photos. (Those are the "Harry" and "Potter" elements of the "Harry Potter Can Fly" mnemonic.) Remember every image you and your students find online IS most likely copyrighted, unless it is specifically licensed as "public domain."

If homegrown or public domain images are not available for your image needs, turn to searchable websites with Creative Commons licensed images next. Several outstanding (and free) websites I recommend are:

1. Flickr Creative Commons: http://flickr.com/creativecommons (also available in the Flickr Advanced Search options: www.flickr.com/search/advanced

2. Compfight: http://compfight.com

3. Wylio: http://wylio.com

4. Behold: http://www.behold.cc

Flickr (www.flickr.com) is a popular photo sharing website with millions of images and an excellent source for photos to use in multimedia projects because:

1. **Clear usage rights**: Photo owners and publishers on Flickr can specifically license images under Creative Commons, removing (in most cases) ambiguity about ownership and attribution credit for photos

2. **Multiple sizes available**: Photos are automatically resized on the site making it easy to download a version appropriate to your purpose, without using secondary image editing software

3. **Owner contact facilitated**: Photo owners can be contacted through the site's messaging feature, if desired, to ask questions and obtain explicit permissions for image reuse (like commercial use) not permitted by the the published license

Content filtering on school networks is an extremely important topic which should be addressed in the context of "digital citizenship" in addition to Internet safety. Please see the appendix at the end of this book, "Balanced Content Filtering in Schools," for resources and suggestions on these issues.

Flickr Creative Commons Image Searching

When searching Flickr for images, do NOT simply search the website from the flickr.com homepage. Image results from that search will NOT be filtered by license. Instead, visit the Flickr Creative Commons page (http://flickr.com/creativecommons) and click the SEE MORE link under the license you want to use. The attribution license is the most permissive, and generally the one I use and recommend others use for media projects.

flickr from YAHOO!

Home   You   Organize & Create   Contacts   Groups   Explore   Upload

Explore / Creative Commons

Many Flickr users have chosen to offer their work under a Creative Commons license, and you can browse or search through content under each type of license.

Here are some recently added bits and pieces:

(i) Attribution License

From goowaa   From Hansel Maneater   From b.roveran   From INOMATA Kentaro   From b.roveran

» 26,523,916 photos (See more)

Click HERE to search for more images shared under this CC license

Next, enter your search terms in the search box at the top of the page. The screenshot below shows the search interface for Flickr images licensed under the Creative Commons Attribution-Only license, accessible on http://www.flickr.com/creativecommons/by-2.0/.

flickr from YAHOO!

Home   You   Organize & Create   Contacts   Groups   Explore   Upload

Explore / Creative Commons / (i)

[SEARCH]

(Or browse popular tags)

Here are the **100 most recent** licensed bits and pieces:

Enter your search terms here!

While this is the simplest way to directly search on Flickr.com for Creative Commons images, the Flickr Advanced Image Search (www.flickr.com/search/advanced) can also be used. Be sure to check the boxes beside "Only search within Creative Commons-licensed content" and "Find content to modify, adapt, or build upon" at the bottom of the Flickr Advanced Search webpage if using it.

☑ Only search within **Creative Commons**-licensed content

☐ Find content to use commercially
☑ Find content to modify, adapt, or build upon

[SEARCH]

Or, return to the basic search without all the knobs and twiddly bits.

www.flickr.com/search/advanced/

If your media project will be used commercially, also check "Find content to use commercially." Use the direct link to search Creative Commons Attribution-Only images (www.flickr.com/creativecommons/by-2.0).

Compfight.com provides another free way to search for Creative Commons licensed content shared on Flickr. License filters must be selected AFTER a keyword search is performed. The screenshot below shows a simple keyword search for "lightning" on Compfight, showing photos with "Any license." Note over 200,000 images are identified with this search.

To filter by Creative Commons license on Compfight.com, click the "Creative commons" link in the left sidebar of the website after performing a keyword search. The screenshot below shows the same, simple keyword search for "lightning" but filtered for Creative

Commons licenses only. Note this time, over 30,000 images are included in search results.

Wylio.com is another website which allows searching of Creative Commons licensed images on Flickr. Unlike the Flickr Creative Commons site and Compfight, however, Wylio requires users to register on the site. Wylio is an ideal image search site when photos will be republished on a blog or other website, because it provides "embed code" including attribution links to the original copyright owner. Embedding can be used to create compound documents which include different types of media as well as text.[93] Only five free photos can be used per month with free accounts, however.

A five minute screencast (www.screenr.com/APY) demonstrating how to use Flickr Creative Commons, Compfight, and Wylio to find

---

[93] Compound document. (n.d.). Wikipedia, the free encyclopedia. Retrieved June 4, 2011, from http://en.wikipedia.org/wiki/Compound_document

and use Creative Commons licensed images in media projects you create along with your students is available on YouTube.[94]

Behold (www.behold.cc) and Simple CC Flickr Search by John Johnson (johnjohnston.info/flickrCC) are other examples of search sites connected to Flickr which make it the premier web resource today for finding Creative Commons licensed media to utilize in projects. These sites along with Joyce Valenza's outstanding hotlist of "copyright-friendly and Copyleft" image sites are included on the Images page of the PlayingWithMedia.com site (http://playingwithmedia.com/pages/images).[95] I will continue to update this page with CC image search sites along with additional resources relating to image use in media projects.

Ending PowerPoint Abuse

"PowerPoint Abuse" is the use of a visual presentation medium (like PowerPoint) as a text-dominated communication tool instead of a visual tool. PowerPoint slide shows, and media presentations more generally, should be dominated by the effective use of VISUAL media rather than text. Garr Reynolds' book "Presentation Zen: Simple Ideas on Presentation Design and Delivery," should be required reading for all media communicators.[96] (That includes you

---

[94] Fryer, W. (2011, February 2). How to find and use Creative Commons images in blog posts - YouTube . YouTube - Broadcast Yourself. . Retrieved July 21, 2011, from http://www.youtube.com/watch?v=ONIagUKG7Vs

[95] Valenza, J. (2007, August 27). Copyright-Friendly and Copyleft (Mostly!). Images and Sound for Use in Media Projects and Web Pages, Blogs, Wikis, etc. Copyright Friendly. Retrieved June 4, 2011, from http://copyrightfriendly.wikispaces.com

[96] Reynolds, G. (2008). Presentation zen: simple ideas on presentation design and delivery. Berkeley, CA: New Riders Pub.

as a reader of "Playing with Media!") Garr is on a personal mission to end "PowerPoint abuse" worldwide. PowerPoint and other multimedia presentation tools like Apple's Keynote were designed as VISUAL software programs, not word processors. Unfortunately, however, many people tend to pack PowerPoint presentations full of text. In many cases, small text fonts are used in PowerPoints which are difficult to read. At times, presenters will actually READ ALOUD full paragraphs of text from their slides to members of an audience. This is usually a bad idea, since people can almost always silently read text faster than a presenter can read it orally. In his "Authors @ Google" presentation, Garr Reynolds summarized many of the key points he made in his book, "Presentation Zen."[97] The free video version on YouTube of the presentation is just over an hour long.

In my most recent "Technology 4 Teachers" course curriculum for pre-service teachers at the University of Central Oklahoma, I included a multi-week focus on Pecha Kucha presentations as well as strategies for finding and using copyright-friendly images.[98] Every teacher in a classroom with Internet access today should be able to effectively find and utilize images within multimedia presentations. "Pecha Kucha presentations" are 20 slide multimedia presentations, narrated for 20 seconds per slide for a total of 6 minutes, 40 seconds. The format was originally invented in Japan for evening events designed to attract young designers interested in networking and learning new ideas.[99] Pecha Kucha presentations are ideal for

[97] Reynolds, G. (2008, March 8). Authors@Google: Garr Reynolds . YouTube - Broadcast Yourself. Retrieved July 2, 2011, from http://www.youtube.com/watch?v=DZ2vtQCESpk

[98] Fryer, W. (2011). Spring 2011 Course Curricula. Technology 4 Teachers by Wesley Fryer at the University of Central Oklahoma. Retrieved July 2, 2011, from http://wiki.wesfryer.com/t4t

[99] Pecha Kucha. (n.d.). Wikipedia, the free encyclopedia. Retrieved July 2, 2011, from http://en.wikipedia.org/wiki/Pecha_Kucha

classroom use because they can provide opportunities for students to develop their oral communication skills utilizing images appropriately in a "Presentation Zen" style.

As a strategy to introduce my college students to both the definition of "PowerPoint abuse" as well as specific strategies for overcoming it, I show them Don McMillian's 4 minute and 24 second comedy routine excerpt, "Life After Death By PowerPoint."[100] (If you choose to show this to students, be warned Don does use the world "hell" in the video.) This video is an outstanding example of how humor can be used effectively to make a serious point. Don has also published a revision of this presentation, "Life After Death by Powerpoint 2010."[101] (9.5 minutes on YouTube.) In the world of business as well as education, multimedia presentations can be poorly created and poorly shared. As digitally savvy educators, it's part of our job to make sure we and our students are not counted among the throngs of "PowerPoint abusers" around the world.

In his book "Brain Rules: 12 Principles for Surviving & Thriving at Work, Home, & School," author John Medina shares twelve rules relevant to us as multimedia communicators.[102] (www.brainrules.net) Rule #4 is: "We don't pay attention to boring things." Rule #10 is:

---

[100] McMillian, D. (2008). Don McMillan: Life After Death by PowerPoint. YouTube - Broadcast Yourself. Retrieved July 2, 2011, from http://www.youtube.com/watch?v=lpvgfmEU2Ck

[101] McMillian, D. (2009). Life After Death by Powerpoint 2010. YouTube - Broadcast Yourself. . Retrieved July 3, 2011, from http://www.youtube.com/watch?v=KbSPPFYxx3o

[102] Medina, J. (2008). Brain rules: 12 principles for surviving and thriving at work, home, and school. Seattle, Wash.: Pear Press.

"Vision trumps all other senses."[103] Effective educators with access to multimedia utilize large, full-screen images during presentations to enhance both learner engagement as well as understanding of concepts. If we understand how the brain works (and we all should as professional educators) we cannot ignore the importance and value of effective image use to support learning.

Whether you are a classroom teacher, a school administrator, or anyone else interested in more effectively communicating with media, I encourage you to embrace the "Presentation Zen" model of using large images with minimal text with PowerPoint or Keynote. Join Garr Reynolds, Don McMillan, Darren Kuropatwa, and me in our work to put an end to "PowerPoint Abuse" through education and presentation coaching following models like "Pecha Kucha." It's important our students learn to become effective multimedia presenters utilizing images to their full, powerful effect. This may be one of the most important lessons you share with your students. It's importance will only increase as we move further into an age saturated with media and information channels. Those individuals best able to command and maintain attention in a media-drenched environment will be those who understand and model effective use of visual media.

Inserting Images Into Media Presentations

Once you have located an image on the Internet to use in a media presentation, there are two basic ways to save and insert it:

1. **Copy and paste**: Right click the image in your web browser (control-click if on a Mac without a two button mouse) and

---

[103] Kuropatwa, D. (2011). Design Matters v4. SlideShare: Upload & Share PowerPoint presentations and documents. Retrieved July 2, 2011, from http://www.slideshare.net/dkuropatwa/design-matters-v4

choose COPY from the contextual menu. Next, navigate to the slide or other location in your media project where you want to include the copied image. Right click (control click on a Mac) and choose PASTE to add the image.

2. **Save and insert**: Right click the image in your web browser (control-click if on a Mac without a two button mouse) and choose SAVE IMAGE AS from the contextual menu. Depending on the web browser used, this option may be called something similar like DOWNLOAD IMAGE AS. After selecting it, choose the folder (or create the folder initially) where you want to save your project images. Choose a relevant title for the image before saving it to your local hard drive. Next, navigate to the slide or other location in your media project where you want to include the copied image. The menu location of the "Insert Image from File" option in PowerPoint and other media programs varies depending on the version used. Some versions include INSERT as a choice on the software's top menu bar. PICTURE can then be selected, followed by FROM FILE.

When resizing an image in PowerPoint or other media programs, often if you hold down the SHIFT key the image will retain its original proportions. This prevents images from becoming distorted due to mis-proportioned resizing.

Regardless of the method selected to add an image to a media project, it is VITAL to save the URL (website address) where the image was obtained AT THE TIME it is either saved or copied. If not, it is often impossible to relocate the original source website when creating a bibliography / Works Cited page. The following methods can be used to save image sources for later use in a documentation page or footnotes.

1. **Word processing file**: Save the image URL in a text editor file or word processing file when you copy or save it initially. If this text document is saved on a cloud-based service, like Google

Docs or Evernote, it can be accessed from any Internet-connected computer. It's often easier to save the website address in a locally saved text document, however. TextWrangler is an excellent, free text editor on Apple / Macintosh computers.[104] (It has powerful search/replace capabilities.) A standard word processing program like Microsoft Word or OpenOffice Writer (free) can be used also.

2. **Social bookmarks tag**: Social bookmarks are website "favorites" or bookmarks which are saved in the cloud, on an Internet server, instead of being saved on a local hard drive. Diigo (www.diigo.com) and delicious (www.delicious.com) are two of my favorites, but many other options are also available including Google Bookmarks (www.google.com/bookmarks). When saving a social bookmark, users can assign a title, description, and "tags" to the saved website. When conducting research for a specific assignment or paper, it is possible to use a special tag when saving images as well as other web resources for later reference. Linking to or clicking on that tag within your social bookmarks account will display only a list of those saved websites.

3. **Website archive**: Websites like Imagestamper (www.imagestamper.com) function similar to social bookmarking sites, keeping links to utilized images "in the cloud" on a server accessible from any Internet-connected computer. Imagestamper, however, also records the Creative Commons license terms (if provided) for utilized images at the time it is saved to a user's

---

[104] TextWrangler. (n.d.). Bare Bones Software. Retrieved July 3, 2011, from http://www.barebones.com/products/textwrangler/

account.[105]   This can become documentation proving the licensing terms of the image at the time you copy or save it, in the event they change or the image is removed from the website in the future.

4. **Bibliographic web tool**: A variety of web-based citation assistance tools are available, which not only provide formatting for bibliographies using different standards (MLA, APA, etc.) but also save cited websites online in a user's profile account. I used BibMe (www.bibme.com) to create the citations for this book project. Commercial tools like NoodleTools (www.noodletools.com) can be licensed for use in an entire school or school district, and provide web-based bibliographic tools for images as well as other online resources.[106]

The citation process is never a favorite part of multimedia projects or research papers for students. It's a vital element, however, since students can learn about intellectual property rights as well as attribution aspects of Creative Commons licensing as they create bibliographies. In our digital era, students should NEVER hand-copy URLs / websites onto paper for later keyboarding into a works cited page. Digital content should be digitally attributed. I invite you to play with some of the bibliographic resources included in this

---

[105] Dale, J. (2011, June 14). How can new technology support teaching and learning? Integrating ICT into the MFL classroom. Retrieved July 3, 2011, from http://joedale.typepad.com/integrating_ict_into_the_/2011/06/how-can-new-technology-support-teaching-and-learning.html

[106] Valenza, J. (2009, December 7). GETTING STARTED KEYNOTE: The Wizard of Apps. K12 Online Conference 2010. Retrieved July 3, 2011, from http://k12onlineconference.org/?p=443

section, and share some of them with your students. While the names and specific steps required to use these different tools will change with time, our need to digitally attribute sources for images as well as other online resources will remain persistent. This is an example of what I call a "transcendent digital skill." Appropriately and efficiently citing digital resources is an important aspect of our work as academics and scholars. Fortunately, digital tools like those described here can make this process MUCH less time consuming.

For more inspiration about digital citation tools as well as other wonderful applications for 21st century learners, check out Joyce Valenza's amazing keynote for the K-12 Online Conference, "The Wizard of Apps." Joyce's accompanying "New Tools Workshop Wiki" (newtoolsworkshop.wikispaces.com) is one of the best compilations of digital tools for learning you'll find anywhere. Joyce has created a revised version of this website for 2011 worth checking out on sdst.libguides.com/newtools.

A variety of copyright friendly and "copyleft" image resources are linked on the Storychasers' Image Resource wiki page (info.storychasers.org/home/resources/images).

Photo 365 Projects

Up to this point in this chapter we have focused attention on resources and strategies for finding and using images created by others. Now I'd like to turn to ideas and resources for creating "homegrown" images as well as remixes, or "derivative works," of images shared by others.

Aristotle is frequently misquoted as the author of the statement, "We are what we repeatedly do. Excellence, then, is not an act, but a habit." While this statement originated with Will Durant's 1926 book, The Story of Philosophy: The Lives and Opinions of the World's Greatest Philosophers, the paraphrase of this concept from

Aristotle in "Nicomachean Ethics" is true to the spirit of his words.[107] In the context of "playing with media" and creating images, this Aristotelian advice can be paraphrased simply: "Take lots of pictures." To this exhortation I'd append, "...and share them with others."

Take lots of pictures and share them with others. This is a recipe for developing not only digital photographic skills, but also "the eye of a photographer" always looking at the world for interesting subjects, scenes, and angles.

Splendid Rotunda by Wesley Fryer [108]

---

[107] Aristotle. (n.d.). Wikiquote. Retrieved July 3, 2011, from http://en.wikiquote.org/wiki/Aristotle

[108] Fryer, W. (2011, June 13). 64/365/2011 Splendid Rotunda. wes' 365 photos. Retrieved July 3, 2011, from http://365.wesfryer.com/post/6522218459/164-365-2011-splendid-rotunda-365photos

The availability of camera phones as well as smartphones capable of running photography apps is ushering in a new golden age for photography. Remember the era of film-based photography? In those days, many amateur photographers had to selectively choose which scenes to capture on a family vacation because the number of available exposures on a roll of film was limited. While flash memory cards in today's digital cameras still have a finite capacity, the explosion in memory storage and continued erosion of digital storage costs have changed opportunities for photography with digital tools in fundamental ways.

I encourage you to start a "Photo 365 Project" as soon as possible. Photo365 projects involve taking at least one picture each day, and sharing one photograph on a special website or with a special webservice to aggregate, archive, and share your images. Inspired by Bob Sprankle, Cheryl Oakes, Alan Levine, and Dean Shareski, I started a Photo365 project in 2011 (365.wesfryer.com). Although I sometimes have to "catch up" when I miss a day or two, generally I have found the commitment to post an image for every day of the year as a worthwhile challenge that keeps my mind thinking regularly about photography.

As discussed earlier in the book, I believe the personal use of digital tools is essential for us as teachers. The two essential elements required to finish a project are TIME and a DEADLINE. Photo365 projects can provide regular incentive as well as accountability to other people "following" your 365 project to become a more competent photographer through regular practice. While different groups are available to share 365 project images, like the "2011/365photos" group on Flickr and 365project.org, the most important things to do are commit to the project and select an online space for sharing your images. 365project.org identifies five primary reasons to participate in a Photo 365 project:

1. Improve your photography skills

2. Capture otherwise forgotten moments in your life

3. Easier than writing a diary or blog

4. Only takes a few minutes each day

5. Facebook App to make sharing easy

In the context of "Playing with Media," we can add: "Develop media creation and sharing skills which will benefit my students in the classroom." Photo365 projects are not only fun and personally rewarding, but they also develop the skills we need as teachers to more effectively work with images with our students.

In the January 6, 2011, episode of the Seedlings webcast, guests and hosts discussed photo 365 projects as well as applications for capturing and sharing smartphone photos.[109] The idea of a Classroom "Photo 180" project was put forward. This would be a "Photo365" style project and website, but the target dates would be 180 days which comprise the days in the academic year. Instead of posting photos as the teacher, students could rotate having responsibility for posting a single image each day to the Photo180 blog which reflected something which was studied or learned that day. While hundreds of classrooms around the world are using blogs today, I have not seen any teachers start a Photo180 project. If you start one or know of someone who has started one, please let me know and share it on Twitter using the hashtag, #playingwithmedia.

---

[109] Sprankle, B., Oakes, C., & Barr, A. (2011, January 6). Seedlings @ Bit By Bit Podcast.Show 102: Photo 365 Projects. Retrieved July 3, 2011, from http://bobsprankle.com/bitbybit_wordpress/?p=2828

Quickshare Sites

A variety of websites and smartphone applications are available today which facilitate "quicksharing" of photos as well as other types of media online. Many of these websites also integrate with social media sites like Twitter and Facebook, further facilitating the fast sharing of images along with short commentaries. Some of these popular quickshare sites also offer free smartphone applications for iOS and Android devices. Many support uploading and sharing photos via email, making them ideal for use with an email-capable cell phone camera. Examples include:

1. Yfrog (yfrog.com)

2. TwitPic (twitpic.com)

3. Instagram (instagr.am)

4. Tumblr (www.tumblr.com)

Yfrog.com is a "quickshare" photo site tightly integrated with Twitter. The following image was taken and shared by Aysem Bray, a Spanish teacher in South Korea. In case you don't read Spanish, the translated note in English says, "Spanish is the best class in the school."[110]

---

[110] Bray, A. (2011, June 8). Aysem_Bray Status Update. Twitter. Retrieved June 24, 2011, from http://twitter.com/Aysem_Bray/status/78671945410949120

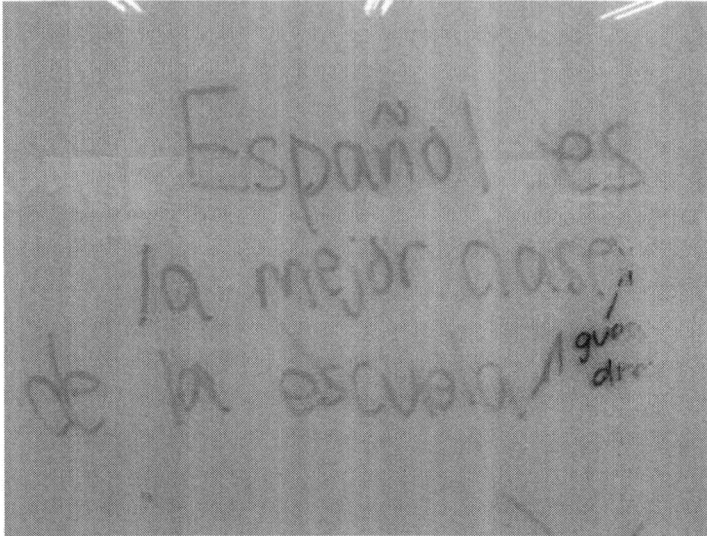

@Aysem_Bray
Aysem Bray

I love my students... # kispd, #ade2011
yfrog.com/h8oqawej

YFrog   flag this media

8 Jun via Twitter for iPhone   ☆ Favorite ⇄ Retweet ↰ Reply

Websites like these can enable teachers as well as students to document their learning and experiences throughout the day more frequently and with greater immediacy than was possible in past decades. We live in an era of burgeoning "citizen journalism," and this prospect is potentially disruptive within our schools as well as traditional, mainstream media channels.

TwitPic (twitpic.com) caught the attention and grabbed the imagination of millions of people in January 2009 when Janis Krums snapped a photo of a U.S. Airways Airbus plane which had just landed in the Hudson River.

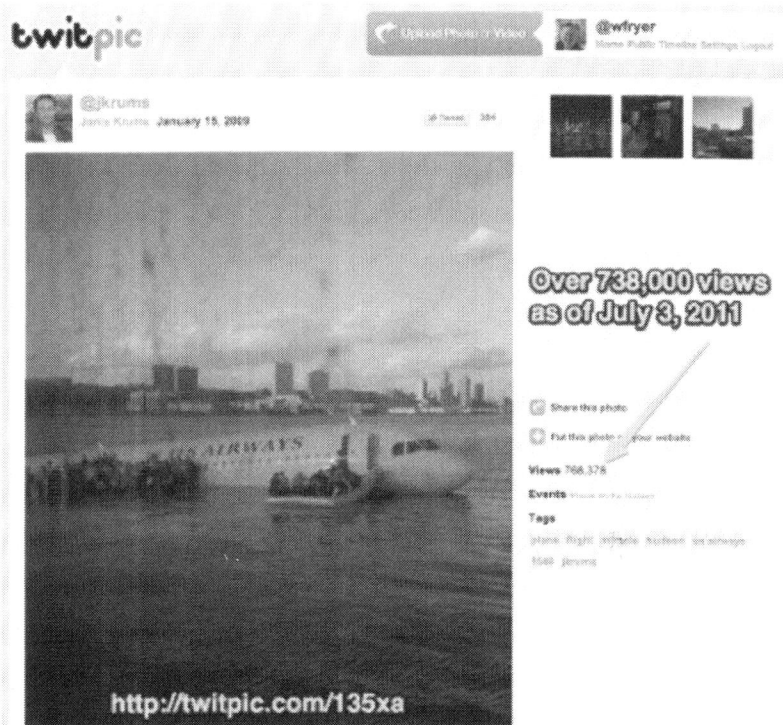

"There's a plane in the Hudson" by Janis Krums [111]

Janis was able to readily share this dramatic photo for a variety of reasons:

1. He had a smartphone with a camera in his pocket
2. He had previously setup an account with TwitPic and had his smartphone "prepped" (with the appropriate email address or an application) to post there

---

[111] Krums, J. (2009, January 9). There's a plane in the Hudson.Twitpic - Share photos and videos on Twitter. Retrieved July 3, 2011, from http://twitpic.com/135xa

3. He was in a location with 3G cell tower data connectivity, permitting the upload

Like Janis, we can each become prepared to document events in our life (including our classroom learning experiences) using a Smartphone and quicksharing sites. While I don't recommend TwitPic as a sharing site for a Photo365 project, I think it is a great site and service to potentially utilize. TwitPic's revised "terms of service" caused a loud flap in May 2011 when the company attempted to lay a comprehensive intellectual property claim to user photographs.[112] This situation highlighted the importance of users being aware of photo sharing site terms. It also revealed the potential for vocal citizen journalists as well as larger social media channel organizations to put pressure on organizations to change their policies when they stray far out of line. TwitPict is a good, free iOS application for posting images directly to TwitPic.

Instagram (instagr.am) is another website popular with smartphone photographers because of its free iOS application as well as the community which has grown around its service. According to a May 2011 presentation by the Instagram co-founder, Kevin Systrom, the site was supporting four million users worldwide who were posting ten photos per second, on average. Not bad for a company with only four employees![113] The Instagram smartphone application not only permits photo capture and uploading, but also includes a variety of filter effects to adjust images directly on an

---

[112] Fleishman, G. (2011, May 12). All Your Pics Are Belong to Us: at image hosting services, Terms and Conditions always apply. Boing Boing. Retrieved July 3, 2011, from http://boingboing.net/2011/05/12/all-your-pics-are-be.html

[113] Instagram's instant growth. (2011, May 24). CNNMoney Tech Tumblr . Retrieved July 3, 2011, from http://cnnmoneytech.tumblr.com/post/5806027102/instagrams-instant-growth

iPhone, iPod Touch, or iPad before sharing them. It integrates well with a variety of social networking sites including Facebook, Twitter, Foursquare, and Posterous. Instagram website community members can rate and comment on the photographs of others from directly in the application. Instagram is a good choice for Photo365/Photo180 projects.

Tumblr (www.tumblr.com) is officially called a "micro-blogging" website, used by millions to share photos, text, and other kinds of media. The explosive growth of Tumblr as a media sharing site was summarized well in the article on TechCrunch: "All Of July 2009: Tumblr Did 250 Million Pageviews. May 16, 2011: Tumblr Did... 250 Million Pageviews."[114] The simplicity of Tumblr makes it an ideal "Quickshare" site for images. Photos can be posted to Tumblr with a private, special email address unique to your account, via the website interface, or via the free Tumblr smartphone application. The screenshot below shows different posting options in the Tumblr app for iPhone: text, photo, quote, link, chat, audio or video.

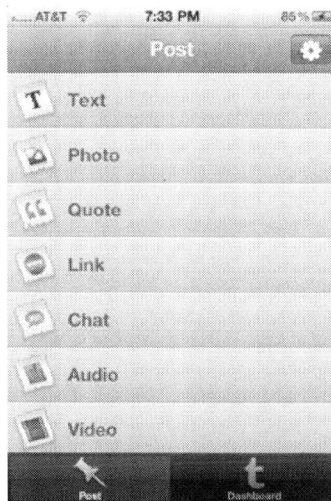

---

[114] Siegler, M. (2011, May 17). All Of July 2009: Tumblr Did 250 Million Pageviews. May 16, 2011: Tumblr Did... 250 Million Pageviews. TechCrunch. Retrieved July 3, 2011, from http://techcrunch.com/2011/05/17/tumblr-pageviews-a-day/

I chose Tumblr as a free website for my 365 Photos project in 2011 to learn more about how the site works along with different available tools for mobile-posting content. Since Tumblr lets any user "map" their website to a custom domain, I was able to make the public address of my 365 project 365.wesfryer.com instead of wfryer.tumblr.com. This process requires a change to the "DNS record" of your registered domain as well as your Tumblr blog settings.[115] This process basically makes your site look a bit "fancier" and more professional, since it's tied to your own domain, but functionally it doesn't enhance or change the site.

Don't pay more than about $12 US if you are purchasing a domain name to use. Prices for domains vary widely, and it's pretty easy to get ripped off. I have most of my domains registered via GoDaddy.com, and find it helpful to have most of my domains with the same registrar to keep track of renewal dates.

TwitPic, Instagram and Tumblr are examples of quicksharing sites I recommend. The screenshot below shows my current iPhone applications in my "upload" category, which include blogging as well as photo sharing sites.

---

[115] Using a custom domain name. (n.d.). Tumblr. Retrieved July 3, 2011, from http://www.tumblr.com/docs/en/custom_domains

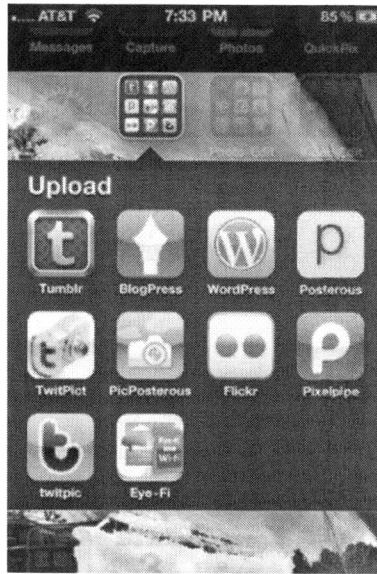

iOS Upload Apps by Wesley Fryer [116]

While some of these websites and web services will undoubtedly change in the months and years ahead, I am confident "quicksharing" sites and tools will remain as a category of available web services. Mobile media sharing is a game changer for many reasons, but principally because it supports "the ethic of minimal clicks." With a few touches on my smartphone, I can take a photo, post it online, and notify people "following" my site or my other social media accounts (like Facebook and Twitter) about the immediate, global availability of this image. Who would have imagined even ten years ago, much less a century or more ago, that so many people in our society would have this kind of publishing power literally at their fingertips and in their pockets. We need to "play with media" on our own and with students to better

---

[116] Fryer, W. (2011). iOS Uploading Apps for Blogging & Photosharing (3 July 2011). Flickr - Photo Sharing. Retrieved July 3, 2011, from http://www.flickr.com/photos/wfryer/5898852799/

understand the capabilities as well as responsibilities which are inherent in these digital communication technologies.

It's not enough to tell young people, "Make good choices with your phone." We need to participate in social media publishing, sharing, tagging, and collaboration with others to remain relevant mentors as well as educators in our digital communication age. Young as well as older people need to practice responsible media sharing. Photo365 and Photo180 projects can provide frequent opportunities to have the conversations we need to develop responsible digital citizens in our classrooms, homes and communities.

Using Posterous to Share Images

Posterous is another "quickshare" or "micro-blogging" website and service. As described in the preceding chapter on "Digital Text," it is an ideal website for teachers and students to use collaboratively since it permits both post and comment moderation, AND supports rich media publication via email attachments.

The screenshot below is a post on my 5 Photo Story Posterous blog, accessible on 5photos.posterous.com.

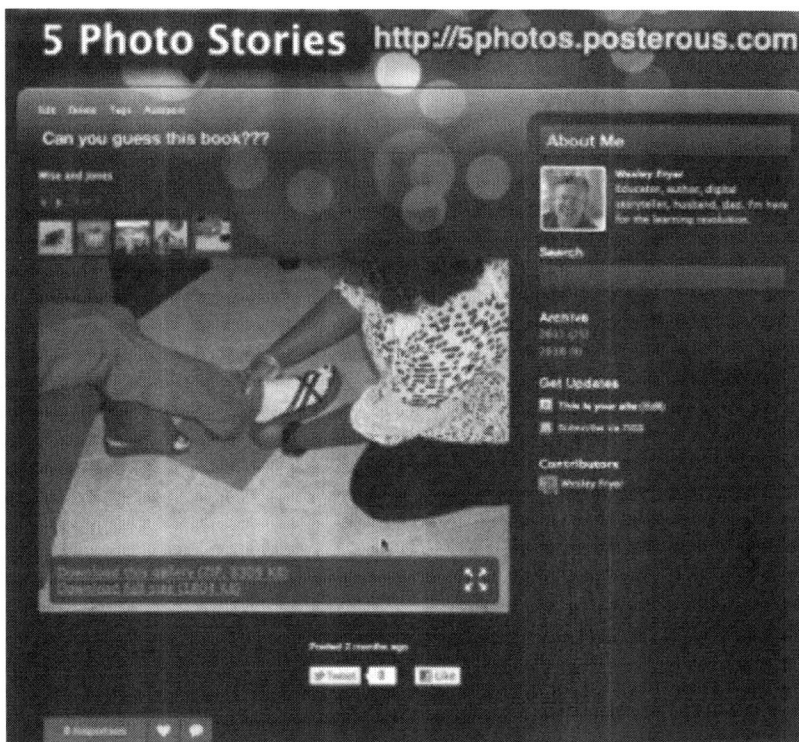

In media workshops, I sometimes challenge participants to create short stories using only five images. In the case of the post shown above, I challenged participants to tell the story of a fairy tale using just photos, as a 5 photo story "charades" activity. This idea had its genesis with two educators. Karen Montgomery started the Flickr group "Tell a Story with 5 Photos for Educators" several years ago, and I've enjoyed sharing and encouraging other people to create 5 photo stories ever since.[117] As of this writing, this open group (you're welcome to join) includes over seventy "five photo stories" about a wide range of topics. The story "Getting a New Haircut," which

---

[117] Montgomery, K. (2007). Flickr Group: Tell a Story with 5 Photos for Educators. Flickr - Photo Sharing. Retrieved June 23, 2011, from http://www.flickr.com/groups/fivephotos/

features my younger daughter (Rachel, the illustrator of "Playing With Media") is definitely my favorite.[118] With encouragement from Karen, I later worked with Rachel to turn that photo story into a VoiceThread ("Getting a New Haircut") which has been viewed over 64,000 times. The idea of creating five photo stories as "fairy tale charades" was an idea Curby Alexander shared with me in the fall of 2010 when we taught "Computers in the Classroom" as adjunct instructors together at the University of North Texas.

Posterous creates a visually pleasing image gallery as a browseable carousel when someone emails multiple photos as attachments to the same email, sent to "yourblogname@posterous.com." This is not only possible using a web browser and any webmail interface supporting email attachments, but also using iOS devices like an iPhone. To send multiple attachments in the same email to a Posterous blog (or another destination) open the Photos application on your iPhone. Instead of clicking on an individual photo, touch select the publish arrow in the upper right corner of the screen.

---

[118] Fryer, W. (2007). Getting a new haircut! in Tell a Story with 5 Photos for Educators. Flickr - Photo Sharing. Retrieved June 23, 2011, from http://www.flickr.com/groups/fivephotos/discuss/72157601453847579/

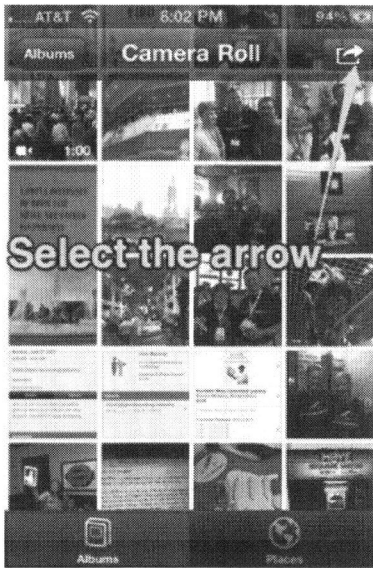

Next, touch select all the photos you would like to share via email to a Posterous blog.

Then click the SHARE button in the lower left corner, and choose to email the photos. All the photos you select will be sent as attachments to the SAME email address. This is a great technique to utilize with students using camera-equipped iPod Touches, iPads, or iPhones.

I challenge you to create a free blog site on Posterous.com and experiment posting multiple photos to it using email attachments. Do not underestimate the importance and power of "the ethic of minimal clicks!" Since sharing images to "quickshare" sites like Tumblr and Posterous requires fewer clicks, teachers as well as students can be empowered to share MORE visual content as well as other forms of media there. This is a good thing (particularly on a Posterous site which you can MODERATE as the teacher) for many reasons. As you create your own sites for photo sharing and Photo365/Photo180 projects, please share the links on Twitter using the #playingwithmedia hashtag as well as on the Playing with Media Facebook page!

Free Image Editing and Drawing Software Options

A variety of free and open source software programs are available which support image editing as well as digital drawing which should be installed on all the computers at your school.

For younger students, TuxPaint (tuxpaint.org) is an open source drawing program similar to commercial programs like KidPix. TuxPaint is a bitmap-based drawing program which allows students to create a variety of creative artwork. It is available for Windows, Macintosh and Linux computers. Since it's open source, it is completely free for anyone to use and does not require a software license.

The Gimp (www.gimp.org) is an open source image editing and manipulation program which has capabilities similar to (but not nearly as advanced as) Adobe PhotoShop. Like TuxPaint, the Gimp is available for Windows, Macintosh and Linux computers. On the Apple / Macintosh platform, I've found the open source program SeaShore (seashore.sourceforge.net) to be extremely user friendly and powerful. SeaShore is based in part on the Gimp, but is not as fully featured. While I would never pretend to be a gifted professional image designer, I have been pleased with the kinds of images I've been able to create with these free programs. 2006 was the last year I had access, via a software license purchased by my employer, to the full version of Adobe PhotoShop.

In the world of image editing and drawing, there are two basic types of programs: pixel-based image editors (like PhotoShop, the Gimp and SeaShore) and vector based drawing applications. Adobe Illustrator is an example of a professional, vector-based drawing application. Inkscape (inkscape.org) is an open source, vector-based drawing application with capabilities similar to Illustrator. When drawings are created in a vector-based software program, they can be scaled as desired (made very large or very small) without the image losing its resolution. Keep Inkscape in mind for yourself and students who are interested in creating vector-based illustrations but may not have the funds required to purchase a commercial software license for a program like Illustrator.

The ability to capture and annotate screenshots on my computer screen is essential for me as a blogger and multimedia communicator. Skitch (skitch.com) is my favorite application on the Apple / Macintosh platform for screencapture and annotation. I love how Skitch supports direct uploading to Flickr. Although a commercial version of Skitch is now available, I continue to be happy using the free version. Although Apple / Macintosh computers support available keyboard shortcuts for creating screenshots, I've found the flexibility and power of Skitch far exceeds those options.[119] On the Windows side, Zscreen (code.google.com/p/zscreen) is an open source, free screen capture tool which supports direct uploads to Flickr as well as other sites. It does not support flexible image annotation and drawing tools like Skitch, however. Windows7 computers include the built-in "Snipping Tool" application for creating screenshots.[120]

iPhoneography

Smartphone photography can be amazing. The image below is one of my all-time favorite iPhoneography examples. Less than sixty seconds after I took this photo, this block of melting snow and ice broke off from the roof of our home in Oklahoma in February 2011. If I hadn't had my iPhone in my pocket with the HDR photo option enabled, I wouldn't have been able to capture and archive this moment!

---

[119] Mac OS X: Shortcuts for taking pictures of the screen. (2004, June 21). Apple Support. Retrieved July 3, 2011, from http://docs.info.apple.com/article.html?artnum=61544

[120] Use Snipping Tool to capture screen shots . (n.d.). Windows home - Microsoft Windows. Retrieved July 3, 2011, from http://windows.microsoft.com/en-US/windows-vista/Use-Snipping-Tool-to-capture-screen-shots

"Before the Fall" by Wesley Fryer [121]

iPhoneography is a portmanteau of the words "iPhone" and "photography." Flickr groups (www.flickr.com/groups/iphoneography) and websites (www.iphoneography.com) dedicated to iPhoneography continue to gain popularity as the image capture as well as editing capabilities of the iPhone have improved. For me, my iPhone4 was the first high definition camcorder anyone in our family owned. That was significant, but the fact that my iPhone4 is almost always in my pocket makes it the best camera I've ever owned. A camera is not useful if it is not available when you need to take a photograph. I love photography and I love using my iPhone, so the allure of iPhoneography to me should be readily apparent.

---

[121] Fryer, W. (2011, February 20). Before the Fall. Flickr - Photo Sharing. Retrieved July 3, 2011, from http://www.flickr.com/photos/wfryer/5462802696/in/set-72157626097188874/

Photography Apps for iPhoneography [122]

The best website I've found to date for sharing favorite mobile applications is Appolicious.com, thanks to Illinois educator Lucy Gray. I created a new list of my favorite ten iPhoneography apps as of July 2011, which is linked to each respective app.[123] These include applications for HDR (high dynamic range) photography, panoramic photos, and rapid fire / burst mode photography.

---

[122] Fryer, W. (2011). Photography Capture Apps for iPhoneography. Flickr - Photo Sharing. Retrieved June 26, 2011, from http://www.flickr.com/photos/wfryer/5875208043/

[123] Fryer, W. (2011, July 3). iPhoneography Capture Apps (Jul 2011) by wfryer. Appolicious App Directory. Retrieved July 3, 2011, from http://www.appolicious.com/curated-apps/3578-iphoneography-capture-apps-jul-2011

For a much more detailed exploration of iPhoneography and iPhone photo apps, check out Stephanie Robert's book: The Art of iPhoneography: A Guide to Mobile Creativity. (www.artofiphoneography.com)

VoiceThread Digital Stories

Of all the websites I've tried and used with students to share media, VoiceThread.com is my favorite. VoiceThread is unique as a web-based, image and audio sharing website because of the way it permits people to interactively comment with text, audio and video on photographs as well as videos shared in a "slideshow-like" presentation. The way it allows VoiceThread creators to moderate comments is very important for classroom teachers. An educational version of VoiceThread is available on ed.voicethread.com, with free as well as paid versions of accounts available. The best way to understand VoiceThread is to watch an example of a student project. A two minute screencast of a VoiceThread created by my older daughter in third grade, when she created a book report about Helen Keller, is available on YouTube. [124]

In addition to demonstrating the basics of VoiceThread, this example also highlights the power of public sharing and moderated commenting using VoiceThread. The person who shared the first comment on the last slide of this VoiceThread was Sarah's grandfather, Tom Fryer. Unless Sarah had recorded and digitally shared this book report online, it is doubtful her grandfather would have ever had an opportunity to listen to her or provide direct, specific feedback about her project. Media projects and VoiceThread digital stories do not have to "go viral" to have a significant impact on the learners who create them as well as the extended families which support those learners. This VoiceThread project is not only an example of a "21st Century Book Report," it's also a case study in how digital portfolios can be powerful tools for assessment, growth, and learning within a community. More examples of book reports

---

[124] Fryer, S. (2010, March 24). A VoiceThread about Helen Keller - YouTube . YouTube - Broadcast Yourself. Retrieved July 21, 2011, from http://www.youtube.com/watch?v=I3vYmKg3aww

created with VoiceThread are linked on the "Great Book Stories" project on greatbookstories.pbworks.com.

To help you understand how to use VoiceThread to create and share digital stories like Sarah's previous example, I created four, short screencasts. These are available online both on the website Screenr.com (where I initially recorded them) as well as on YouTube.

1. **How to create a new educator account on VoiceThread.com** (available on Screenr and YouTube) [125]

2. **Creating a VoiceThread: Images** (available on Screenr and YouTube) [126]

3. **Creating a VoiceThread: Comments** (available on Screenr and YouTube) [127]

4. **Creating a VoiceThread: Sharing** (available on Screenr and YouTube) [128]

A wealth of superb resources are available which can help you learn more about VoiceThread and the ways it can be creatively utilized in the classroom to support student learning. The V o i c e T h r e a d 4 E d u c a t i o n w i k i

[125] Fryer, W. (2011, January 28). How to create a new educator account on VoiceThread.com. Broadcast Yourself. Retrieved July 21, 2011, from http://www.youtube.com/watch?v=3KZOxlgKIbU

[126] Fryer, W. (2010, January 28). Part 1 of 3: Creating a VoiceThread (images). YouTube - Broadcast Yourself. Retrieved July 21, 2011, from http://www.youtube.com/watch?v=7cyuGg1ORPc

[127] Fryer, W. (2010, January 28). Part 2 of 3: Creating a VoiceThread (comments). YouTube - Broadcast Yourself. Retrieved July 21, 2011, from http://www.youtube.com/watch?v=rzwR9o9dOew

[128] Fryer, W. (2010, January 28). Part 3 of 3: Creating a VoiceThread (sharing). YouTube - Broadcast Yourself. Retrieved July 21, 2011, from http://www.youtube.com/watch?v=Hf1SZ0-duEA

(voicethread4education.wikispaces.com) maintained by Colette Cassinelli is a superb, updated resource with links to numerous classroom project examples using VoiceThread.[129] These are organized by grade level and content area in the left sidebar of the website. Bill Ferriter's website, "Using Voicethread for Digital Conversations" is also excellent and worth checking out.[130]

MindMapping Applications

Mindmapping or concept mapping is an excellent strategy for brainstorming and organizing ideas. In 2003, I published the article, "Inspiration Software: An Essential Tool in Every Classroom" in TCEA's TechEdge magazine.[131] Since that time, my enthusiasm for mindmapping applications has not dwindled but my awareness of software in this "genre" has expanded considerably. While Inspiration (www.inspiration.com) remains one of the best-known commercial software programs for concept mapping, a variety of other options are also available. Rather than provide an exhaustive list of these software options, I want to provide you with a few personal recommendations as well as ideas for learning about additional options.

---

[129] Cassinelli, C. (2011). VoiceThread 4 Education. WikiSpaces. Retrieved July 3, 2011, from http://voicethread4education.wikispaces.com

[130] Ferriter, B. (2010). Using Voicethread for Digital Conversations. Digitally Speaking. Retrieved July 4, 2011, from http://digitallyspeaking.pbworks.com/w/page/17791585/Voicethread

[131] Fryer, W. (2003). Inspiration Software: An Essential Tool in Every Classroom. Tools for the TEKS: Integrating Technology in the Classroom. Retrieved July 4, 2011, from http://www.wtvi.com/teks/02_03_articles/inspiration.html

CMapTools (cmap.ihmc.us,) Freemind (freemind.sourceforge.net) and Xmind (www.xmind.net) are all free concept mapping / mind mapping software program. CMapTools and Freemind are both open source. These are "client-side" applications, which must be downloaded to a local hard drive and installed before using them.

Bubble.us (bubbl.us) is a free web-based (cloud-based) mind mapping platform. The creators of Inspiration software offer a commercial, cloud-based version of their software called MyWebspiration (www.mywebspiration.com.) Both Bubble.us and MyWebspiration permit users to create concept maps within a web browser, and both access and share those mind maps with others using provided hyperlinks.

iPad users can also create and share mind maps using a variety of different applications. My favorite free iOS app for concept mapping is Popplet (popplet.com,) which also has a paid version with the ability to create more than one map. Other iOS mind mapping options include iThoughtsHD, MindNode, and Mindmeister.

As you play with media, including images. remember to utilize different tools for creating and sharing concept maps. WikiPedia has a more extensive list of concept mapping and mind mapping software with links you may want to explore further.[132]

Summary

I hope the ideas and resources included in this chapter have inspired you to "play with images" in new ways. We must embrace the challenges as well as opportunities for CREATING with images in the classroom if we are to effectively prepare our students for the

---

[132] List of concept mapping and mind mapping software. (n.d.).Wikipedia, the free encyclopedia. Retrieved July 4, 2011, from http://en.wikipedia.org/wiki/ List_of_concept_mapping_and_mind_mapping_software

world of TODAY and tomorrow. We live in a media-drenched society, but many people do not actively practice critical thinking skills in response to the media messages which surround us. By making the shift from mere "media consumers" to "media pro-sumers" and content creators, we and our students can develop media literacy skills we not only need to be effective learners but also contributing citizens in our communities, states and nations.

6- Video

Video by Rachel Fryer [133]

---

[133] Fryer, R. (2011, June 26). Video by Rachel Fryer. Flickr - Photo Sharing. Retrieved July 4, 2011, from http://www.flickr.com/photos/wfryer/5875723716/in/set-72157626886284140

Every full length, feature film we watch at the movie theater or on DVD took thousands of hours to create. Videos created by students and other amateur filmmakers can also take many hours to plan, record, edit, and publish. A variety of videography tools are available today, however, which can dramatically simplify and speed up these processes. This chapter highlights ways we can use videos created by others more effectively to support student learning. In addition, it explores a variety of methods and tools you can use with students to create and share your own videos. A variety of student video project examples are included.

Longer, complex video projects can be compelling to watch. However, shorter and simpler videos are more useful and practical in the classroom. Shorter video types highlighted in this chapter are:

1. Narrated Slideshows

2. No-Edit Videos

3. Quick-Edit Videos

4. Screencasts

Best Practices for Showing Video in the Classroom

Although YouTube is still blocked by content filters in many U.S. public schools in 2011, a growing number of school leaders are recognizing the need for balanced approaches to content filtering (balancedfiltering.org.) One step in the process of embracing balanced filtering policies is providing teachers with greater access to Internet content at school than students, including sites like YouTube. In addition to YouTube, other sites like Vimeo (www.vimeo.com), SchoolTube (www.schooltube.com) and TeacherTube (www.teachertube.com) offer a wealth of video content for teachers to utilize with students during classroom lessons.

Whatever the video source might be (even older DVD and VHS videos) the following best practices should be utilized by teachers.

1. Use short clips
2. Ask pre-video questions
3. Download for reliable access
4. Remove Related Distractions

1. Use Short Video Clips

Our brains are wired to receive information in stories and in short rather than long information chunks. It is generally a bad idea to show students an entire, feature-length film in class. Video is used most effectively when it is "chunked" into smaller segments. YouTube videos are limited on "normal" accounts to a maximum length of fifteen minutes. It's a good idea to utilize video in shorter, three to five minute segments, and intersperse the videos with class discussion.

2. Ask Pre-video Questions

Students will be more attentive when you share a video clip if you activate their "anticipatory set" by asking some questions in advance. Provide students with guidance about things to look for in the video or issues which the video segment will raise that you'll discuss together afterwards. Sometimes it is helpful to divide the class into groups, and assign different groups different questions or aspects of the video to focus on. Then provide some group discussion time after the video clip, followed by whole-class sharing and discussion time.

3. Download for Reliable Access

The question of whether or not online videos from sources like YouTube should be downloaded in advance of class has important legal as well as practical aspects. Please refer to the appendix, "Tips for Downloading Web Video," for a more detailed explanation of these issues as well as suggested procedures for web video downloading.

Narrated Slideshows with a Smartphone

Creating videos using recorded video is potentially engaging and challenging, but the process of creating videos with STILL images and audio narration can be an excellent "first phase" for aspiring digital storytellers. A one minute, twelve second video ("The Beach") created by my daughters after they explored a beach in California is available on YouTube. They took included photos with a smartphone and then recorded audio narration for each photo sequentially, the same day they had these experiences and took these photos.[134]

When you shoot video, in contrast to capturing still images or photographs with a camera, there are MANY more considerations to keep in mind and manage. Lighting can be tricky. Audio is harder to capture well with video, but easier to record later during "post-production" editing time. Video file sizes are generally much larger than still image digital photos, resulting in longer transfer as well as upload times. Still image digital storytelling, like the previous example, can allow creators to focus with more intention on the images as well as audio they want to juxtapose in a video. While you and your students may assume "since we've got video recording capabilities, we might as well record videos" I encourage you to

_____

[134] Fryer, S., & Fryer, R. (2011, March 15). The beach (a narrated slideshow created with SonicPics). YouTube - Broadcast Yourself. Retrieved July 12, 2011, from http://www.youtube.com/watch? v=9W3DjgWJtB0

temper that assumption with opportunities to create compelling digital stories with still images and audio first. Most of the approximately 1000 videos shared on the Celebrate Oklahoma Voices learning community are narrated slideshows.[135]

Good iOS applications for creating narrated slideshow digital stories are SonicPics ($2.99) and StoryRobe (99¢). My girls created "The beach" video above using SonicPics. My fifth grade Sunday school students created a series of short videos using the StoryRobe app.[136] The students were able to capture and record these narrated slideshow videos after "storyboarding" and planning their projects. Students were able to plan, record and create their digital stories using StoryRobe in a single 45 minute class. Thanks to StoryRobe and the way it supports "the ethic of minimal clicks," students were able to finish their video projects in a much shorter amount of time than is required for "typical" classroom video projects.

StoryKit is a free iOS application for creating and publishing sequential-page stories, rather than videos. These stories can include images, audio, text, and original artwork. My "Exploring Suzhou, China" video was a digital story created on a train with friends using StoryKit.[137] Like several other storytelling apps, Storykit is sized for

---

[135] Videos. (n.d.). Celebrate Oklahoma Voices! - A learning community empowering digital witnesses of Oklahoma oral history. Retrieved July 12, 2011, from http://lc.celebrateoklahoma.us/video

[136] Fryer, W. (2010, November 14). Initial Christian focused videos with Storyrobe. BLASTcast: A Christian kids podcast and blog from 1st Presbyterian Church in Edmond, Oklahoma. Retrieved July 12, 2011, from http://blastcast.wordpress.com/2010/11/14/initial-christian-focused-videos-with-storyrobe/

[137] Fryer, W. (2010, September 19). Exploring Suzhou, China (a StoryKit mobile phone digital story). Moving at the Speed of Creativity. Retrieved July 12, 2011, from http://www.speedofcreativity.org/2010/09/19/exploring-suzhou-china-a-storykit-mobile-phone-digital-story-learning2cn/

the iPhone/iPod touch but works fine in "2x" (doubled) mode on an iPad. Bernajean Porter, a Colorado educator and well-known digital "storykeeper," has created a more extensive list of iOS applications for digital storytelling on her wiki worth checking out.[138]

A five minute screencast, "Using StoryKit, Storyrobe and Sonic Pics on an iOS Device," is available on YouTube demonstrating how to use these applications and highlights their comparative features. [139] The screencast is also available on Screenr.

No-Edit Videography

Many of the video examples linked in the upcoming section on "Categories of Student Digital Storytelling Projects" took students many hours of work to complete. These kinds of videos, particularly those linked in the "Transformative" category, are powerful messages which connect to audiences emotionally as well as intellectually. These videos can have an impact on our behavior as well as our thinking, and are often difficult to forget. We often find ourselves culturally enriched as a result of watching these videos, or possibly motivated to take action in a new way as a result of their messages.

As much as we might like to ask students to create high quality videos like these on a regular basis, our limited resources sharply restrict the number of time-intensive video projects we can personally complete or assign to others. For these reasons, **I believe**

---

[138] Porter, B. (n.d.). iPad APPS for Storytelling. Storykeepers Resources. Retrieved July 8, 2011, from http://storykeepers.wikispaces.com/iPad+StoryTelling+APPS

[139] Fryer, W. (2010, November 13). Using StoryKit, Storyrobe and Sonic Pics on an iOS Device. YouTube - Broadcast Yourself. Retrieved July 6, 2011, from http://www.youtube.com/watch?v=PKSzIiQ8Xbc

we need to emphasize and model the use of "no-edit" and "quick-edit" videography much more in our classrooms and schools.

A "no-edit" video project is a quickshare: It's a video we capture and share online with others without editing. The video "The Importance of Art Class at School and Creativity" is a favorite personal example and is available on YouTube.[140] I recorded it using my iPhone and directly posted it to YouTube, without editing in iMovie or another software program.

Flash-based camcorders, which do not require tapes for media recording but instead save video files directly to flash-based memory cards or internal memory chips, are ideal for no-edit videography projects. These camcorders are sometimes referred to generically as "Flip cameras," similar to the way tissues are called "Kleenex" by some people. Since Flip cameras are no longer manufactured, it makes sense to use the term "flash-based camcorders" to refer to this camera category rather than "Flip camera." [141] While the Flip brand is on its way out, this category of camera with its specific capabilities as well as limitations is likely to remain a fixture of consumer electronics for many years.

One of the biggest challenges to no-edit videography with a flash-based camcorder is recording video with a high quality AUDIO track. The built-in microphone on most flash-based camcorders is not great, and generally does a poor job filtering out ambient / unwanted audio. For this reason, I recommend purchasing and using flash-based video camcorders which support external microphones.

---

[140] Fryer, R. (2010, November 3). The Importance of Art Class at School and Creativity. YouTube - Broadcast Yourself. Retrieved July 12, 2011, from http://www.youtube.com/watch?v=WkZV-QwpweM

[141] Flip Video. (n.d.). Wikipedia, the free encyclopedia. Retrieved July 5, 2011, from http://en.wikipedia.org/wiki/Flip_Video

These are challenging to find in the consumer video camcorder market, but they are available. One example is the Kodak Playtouch HD camcorder. Flash-based camcorders like this are available for around $150, but may be on sale for less.

Kodak PlayTouch HD Camcorder [142]

Although "no-edit" videography can be a good way to quickly share videos with others, often it's a good idea to at least edit the start and end of recorded videos before uploading them to the web. You can learn to precisely start and stop video recording when a student reporter begins and ends a segment, but it can be helpful to start recording early and stop a little after a "reporter" stops talking. Cutting a recording "too close" can result in the start or end of the

[142] Fryer, W. (2011, May 3). Kodak Playtouch HD Camera.Flickr - Photo Sharing. Retrieved July 4, 2011, from http://www.flickr.com/photos/wfryer/5752595790/in/set-72157626665714083/

video being cut off. For these reasons, "quick-edit videography" should be in your digital toolkit and skill set as a multimedia communicator.

Quick-Edit Videography

"Quick-edit" videography involves a minimal amount of editing before publishing and sharing video online. A three minute video interview with Kristin Hokanson, focusing on copyright and fair use issues for teachers in the classroom, is an example of quick-edit videography available on YouTube.[143] I edited and published this video using iMovie for iPad. Step by step instructions for using iMovie for iPad are in an appendix at the end of this book.

Mobile computing devices like the iPad2 and Android-based tablets equipped with cameras are ideal tools for quick-edit videography. Being able to record video on a mobile device, make edits to the video such as trimming unwanted footage from the start and end of a clip, and adding a theme along with some relevant text links during the movie, is a transformational capability. By "transformational," I mean this is a capability which would not be possible without the enabling technology.

---

[143]Hokansen, K., & Fryer, W. (2011, June 28). Copyright Advice for Teachers from Kristin Hokansen. YouTube - Broadcast Yourself. Retrieved July 14, 2011, from http://www.youtube.com/watch?v=g4rTfZOX-IM

iPad2 Video Interview with iRig Mic by Wesley Fryer [144]

An external microphone like the iRig Mic ($60 - www.ikmultimedia.com/irigmic) can significantly improve the quality of recorded audio. This is an investment well worth making for any classroom or individual who is serious about creating higher quality "quick-edit" videos using iPads, iPhones or iPod Touches. The iRig mic does an excellent job filtering out unwanted, ambient noise in the background during video interviews. People are likely to tolerate poor quality video much more than they will tolerate poor quality audio. If your students are conducting video interviews using an iPad, an iRig (or similar microphone when others are available) should be mandatory to insure audio quality is good.

---

[144] Fryer, W. (2011, May 7). iPad2 Video Interview with iRig Mic. Flickr - Photo Sharing. Retrieved July 6, 2011, from http://www.flickr.com/photos/wfryer/5698109062/in/set-72157626681839756/

At the International Society for Technology in Education (ISTE) conference in Philadelphia, Pennsylvania, I recorded a series of six video interviews using an iPad2, an iRig microphone, and the help of some videographically-skilled friends. These included the previous video interview with Kristin Hokanson. A playlist of these six videos is available on YouTube.[145]

Although you may use a digital camcorder to import and edit video more "traditionally," that process is both time consuming and labor intensive. It is impractical in the classroom on a regular basis, just as it is at a conference. By using a mobile, tablet device like the iPad, this production timeline can be transformed. Touch-tablet

---

[145] Fryer, W. (2011). YouTube Playlist for Voices of #ISTE11. YouTube - Broadcast Yourself. Retrieved July 5, 2011, from http://www.youtube.com/playlist?list=PL342F25AD423CB344

devices permit users to edit, annotate and publish videos on the go. Videos can be edited and shared directly from the device without the need to sync it to another computer. Students can more realistically find the time to share videos "on the go" when using mobile devices. We need to utilize this kind of "quick edit videography" much more in our classrooms and with our students. Quick-edit videography can support both "the ethic of minimal clicks," discussed earlier, and the goal of producing MORE media to learn how to create media of higher quality.

Screencasting

A screencast is a recording of a computer screen with accompanying audio. Sometimes, screencasts include webcam video footage embedded as part of the screencast, shown as a "picture in picture" video. A variety of different software programs and websites are available which enable computer users to record and share screencasts online. A three minute, seventeen second video is a screencast demonstrating how to configure comment moderation on videos you upload to YouTube is available on YouTube.[146]

Salman Kahn, the founder of The Kahn Academy (www.khanacademy.org,) has probably done more to educate people in the United States about "screencasting" than any other individual. Kahn has shared over two thousand screencasts about basic mathematics through advanced Calculus, as well as a variety of other subjects.

Every teacher should understand how to use, create and teach with screencasts. As educators, parents and learners today, we tend to underestimate the value and power of asynchronous sharing. By

[146] Fryer, W. (2011, January 5). How to turn on YouTube video comment moderation. YouTube - Broadcast Yourself.. Retrieved July 12, 2011, from http://www.youtube.com/watch?v=l-KHBleJEhg

permitting learners to choose the time and place where they want to learn, screencasts like those in The Kahn Academy can exemplify the power of asynchronous learning resources.

Many of the referenced videos in this eBook are screencasts. I created most of these using the free website screenr.com, which utilizes browser-based recording. Screencasting using a web browser has several advantages:

1. **Published Online Quickly**: Screenr screencasts are recorded directly on the web so they can be immediately published to the web for online sharing.

2. **No Software to Install**: Since Screenr uses your web browser to make the recording, no software needs to be downloaded and installed to use Screenr.

3. **iOS Compatible**: Some screen recording programs only create Flash-based video files, which are not iOS compatible. Screenr videos can play on any device including iPads, iPhones and iPod Touches.

Since Screenr records directly to the web, it **does** require Internet connectivity to work. This is not a problem for students at universities which provide plenty of bandwidth in classrooms, but this could be a challenge if your school has slower Internet connectivity.

Jing (www.jing.com) is a free, cross-platform screencasting program which teachers should know about and potentially utilize. On the Apple / Macintosh platform, my favorite client-side screencasting program is ScreenFlow. It is $99, however, and like Jing saves screencasts directly to your hard drive which have to be subsequently uploaded to the Internet for online sharing.[147] (The screencast of Rachel's AudioBoo reflection from Pearl Harbor, in the chapter on Audio, was created using ScreenFlow.)

Screencasts can not only be recorded on laptop and desktop computers, but, they can also be recorded and shared from mobile devices like the iPad. The Show Me App (www.showmeapp.com) is an application for iPad which permits teachers, students, and anyone else to directly record screencasts from the iPad using media and resources saved to the device. Lisa Garcia's ShowMe screencast, "The Louisiana Purchase," is an excellent example of the screencasting capabilities of mobile devices like the iPad.[148]

Animated Videos from Text

Animated cartoons can be very time consuming to create. A new genre of websites and software tools is making animated movies much easier to create, however. A one minute, forty second animated video ("MySpace Suicide Prevention") is an example available on YouTube, telling the story of a teacher who helped prevent a teen suicide through his access to the student's MySpace profile page and relationship with the child's parent.[149]

---

[147] Screencasting Software - ScreenFlow Overview. (n.d.).Telestream | Digital video transcoding and workflow solutions. Retrieved July 6, 2011, from http://www.telestream.net/screen-flow/overview.htm

[148] Garcia, L. (2011, June 13). The Louisiana Purchase. ShowMe - The Interactive Learning Community. Retrieved July 6, 2011, from http://www.showmeapp.com/sh/?i=475

[149] Fryer, W. (2011, January 14). MySpace Suicide Prevention. YouTube - Broadcast Yourself.. Retrieved July 11, 2011, from http://www.youtube.com/watch?v=sdsdWn2w194

A variety of websites are now available which permit users to create animated videos using text and offer menu choices for characters and movement. GoAnimate (goanimate.com) and Xtranormal (www.xtranormal.com) are two examples. I created the previous video using Xtranormal for a presentation with Karen Montgomery titled, "Social Media Guidelines for Schools."[150]

Be aware inappropriate videos are created and shared on these sites, so when browsing the sites you or your students may come across content not appropriate for the classroom. A GoAnimate for Schools and Educators (goanimate4schools.com) is available which includes content more carefully monitored and censored for classroom use. Malia Triggs, an elementary teacher in Mississippi, shared a practical presentation at her state educational technology conference titled, "Cartooning Around in Language Arts." Malia uses GoAnimate with her students to support writing skill development and they love it. A forty minute audio podcast of Malia's presentation is available on my blog with more information and resource links from her session.[151]

Categories of Student Digital Storytelling Projects

Humans have been telling stories for millennia. Our brains are wired to remember stories better than we remember lists. One of the

---

[150] Montgomery, K., & Fryer, W. (2011). Social Media Guidelines for Schools. Powerful Ingredients for Blended Learning. Retrieved July 12, 2011, from http://wiki.powerfulingredients.com/Home/workshops/social-media-guidelines

[151] Fryer, W. (2011, February 13). Podcast371: Cartooning Around in Language Arts by Malia Triggs. Moving at the Speed of Creativity. Retrieved July 6, 2011, from http://www.speedofcreativity.org/2011/02/13/podcast371-cartooning-around-in-language-arts-by-malia-triggs-msmeca11/

key, practical lessons we should take away from modern brain research is that as teachers, the more we engage our students in stories as both story consumers and story creators, the more we will help them learn deeply.

It is helpful to explore different examples of student-created videos to gain perspective on the possibilities which digital storytelling offers for classroom learning. These "exemplars" can set a high bar of expectation for the quality student videos, as well as highlight the different ways video can be used to meet academic standards as well as learning objectives in the classroom.

Digital storytelling is a media genre incorporating audio, images, and video to tell stories. Sometimes, videos which are more informational rather than narrative in format are called "digital stories," so the title can be used synonymously with "video." Jason Ohler prefers the term "new media narrative" rather than "digital story" when describing these projects.[152]

The website talkwithmedia.wikispaces.com includes nine categories of student-created digital stories. Most of these are video-based projects. Carol Jordan, a secondary teacher at Shanghai American International School, brainstormed these categories and created this website with me for an extended workshop focused on digital storytelling. On the wiki, we provided links to student video projects in each of the following categories:

1. Audio Podcasts

2. Narrated SlideShow

3. Visual Essay

---

[152] Fryer, W. (2011, June 28). Jason Ohler on Digital Literacy & Digital Storytelling. Moving at the Speed of Creativity. Retrieved July 4, 2011, from http://www.speedofcreativity.org/2011/06/28/jason-ohler-on-digital-literacy-digital-storytelling-iste11/

4. Tutorial

5. Concept Teaching

6. Thinking Out Loud

7. Activity or Event Report

8. Public Service Announcement

9. Transformative

We also created a page of links for Galleries of Student Created Videos, including the following eight websites:

1. Shanghai American School Video Portal (Shanghai, China. This is the school's homegrown YouTube-like site.)

2. SFETT iCan (San Fernando Educational Technology Team - Student Film Festival archives, under the leadership of Marco Torres)

3. Mabry Online Podcasts (Mabry Middle School in Atlanta, GA under the past leadership of Dr. Tim Tyson)

4. Student-created videos from Celebrate Oklahoma Voices (a statewide oral history project sponsored by Storychasers)

5. Center for Digital Storytelling

6. Stories for Change

7. Educational Uses of Digital Storytelling from the University of Houston (see the "Examples" tab)

8. Murmur Toronto (place based storytelling)

The first four sites include student-created videos. The last four may include student examples, but also include adult-created digital stories.

As part of your "Playing with Media" learning journey, I invite you to visit several of these websites and watch some of the videos. Think about the different ways digital stories can be used. Are the nine categories we identified on the "Talk with Media" workshop wiki inclusive of all videos? Why do you think we created a category titled, "Transformative?"

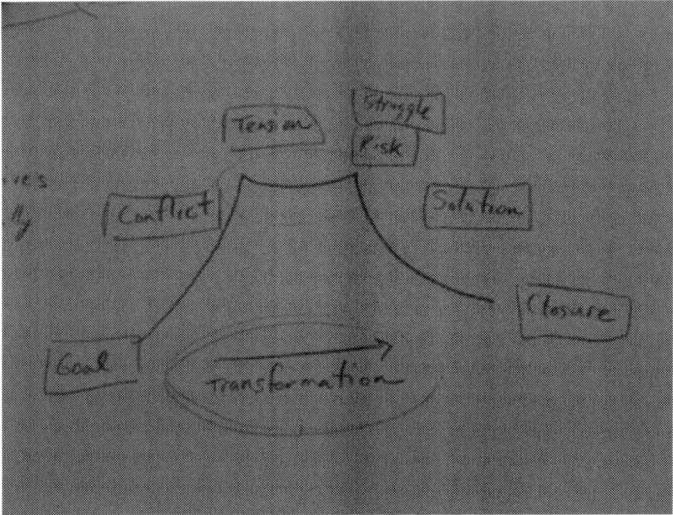

The Story Arc [153]

Video Sandboxes

Schools and school districts serious about digital literacy and helping learners demonstrate the National Educational Technology Standards (ISTE NETS) are providing "homegrown YouTube clone" sites to serve as digital sandboxes for video sharing. These sites

---

[153] Fryer, W. (2010, September 18). The Story Arc, as drawn by a Learning 2.010 Workshop Participant. Flickr - Photo Sharing. Retrieved July 4, 2011, from http://www.flickr.com/photos/wfryer/5000284319/in/set-72157624834948801/

support the public as well as private sharing of online videos, and support linking, embedding, rating and commenting just as YouTube does.

Shanghai International School has a YouTube clone site (portal.saschina.org/video) powered by mediascripts.com.

Tuscaloosa Public Schools, Alabama, has a YouTube clone site (media.tusc.k12.al.us) powered by phpmotion.com.

More schools and school leaders should choose to provide hosted, "YouTube clone" websites like these for students and teachers. While learners at school can certainly publish to free video sharing sites like YouTube (www.youtube.com,) Vimeo (www.vimeo.com,) SchoolTube (www.schooltube.com,) and TeacherTube (www.teachertube.com,) there are many benefits to hosting and running a YouTube clone compared to third-party sites like these. The visibility of videos posted on YouTube can be very beneficial in some circumstances, but it can also be intimidating for people who have not published video online previously. There is a greater perception of safety and protection when publishing video on a local YouTube clone site, even though that video content could be open and accessible to anyone on the Internet.

Just as young children play in a sandbox and learn to build things in a safe environment where it is OK to fail, we need to provide digital sandboxes for learners in our schools creating with media. In the case of video, YouTube clone websites like those described here are the "virtual sandboxes" we need to build and support for teachers as well as students.

Great New Park in Stapleton by Micha Hanson[154]

[154] Hanson, M. (2007, October 6). Great New Park in Stapleton. Flickr - Photo Sharing. Retrieved July 6, 2011, from http://www.flickr.com/photos/denverhansons/1517110434

There are a variety of different companies and solutions in the marketplace offering video hosting and sharing services. I recommend selecting one which has as many features of YouTube as possible. Videos should be:

1. Sharable publicly and privately, but default to PUBLIC

2. Embeddable

3. Viewable on iOS devices (not be flash format only)

4. Linkable

5. Rateable

6. Open for comments

7. Attributed to specific users who upload them

YouTube clone sandbox websites should support and facilitate media sharing, not "media lock-up." Upload settings should default to public, rather than defaulting to private settings, because we want to encourage and support open-web sharing of curricula around the world to support learning locally as well as globally. Ideally, video sharing sites should also support Creative Commons licensing, so materials can be readily reused and remixed by learners in other places. YouTube has added support for optional Creative Commons Attribution-Only licensing.[155] As more educational content is openly licensed and shared on websites like Curriki (www.curriki.org) the less

---

[155] Fryer, W. (2011, June 24). YouTube Now Supports Creative Commons BY Video Licensing #playingwithmedia.Moving at the Speed of Creativity. Retrieved July 6, 2011, from http:// www.speedofcreativity.org/2011/06/24/youtube-now-supports-creative-commons-by-video-licensing-playingwithmedia/

important commercial curricula and textbooks will become in our schools.

Uploading Video to YouTube

Teachers need to be familiar with the process of uploading video to YouTube to become more familiar with the ways YouTube works and how its content can be leveraged effectively for learning in the classroom. Hearing someone talk about or reading about someone who has uploaded to YouTube is insufficient. Experiential learning is required for teachers to understand YouTube. If you have not uploaded to the site previously, create a new, free Google account for yourself (it can be a Gmail address/account or an account tied to an email address you already have) and visit www.youtube.com/upload.

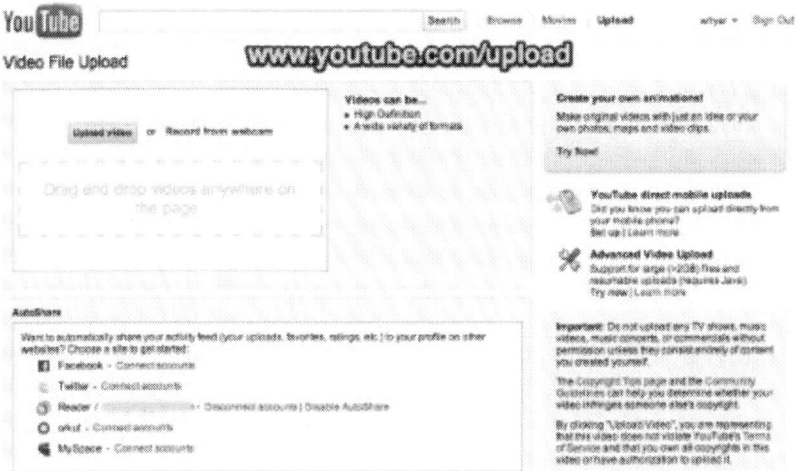

There are many ways to upload video to a YouTube account. The basic way is to click UPLOAD VIDEO from the upload webpage and browse for the video you want to share like an email attachment. Other ways to upload video to YouTube include:

1. Uploading via email, using a custom email address YouTube provides for your account on www.youtube.com/my_videos_mobile_upload.

2. Uploading via a third-party software application, like iPhoto or Picassa

3. Uploading via a third-party websites, like Pixelpipe.com

4. Uploading via a mobile application, like iMovie for iPad

Before you can upload a video from your computer to YouTube with the basic www.youtube.com/upload interface, you need to copy the video from your camera, smartphone, or tablet device onto the local hard drive of your computer. This process is MUCH easier and faster with flash-based camcorders, like the Flip Camera and the Kodak PlayTouch Camera. These cameras have a built-in USB plug which "flips" out and plugs directly into an open USB port on your computer. Like other files on a USB thumb drive (or "jump drive," as some people call it) these video files can be copied from the camera to your local hard drive. Often it's easy to copy them to the desktop first, and later move them into a desired folder on your computer.

The process of saving files from removable storage devices (like a camera or USB drive) and both copying and organizing them into a logical folder structure on your computer is a basic computer skill. It's important to recognize many teachers are not comfortable with this process and need guidance as well as practice to do this. This is why "hands on" workshops about the ideas highlighted in "Playing with Media" are so important. Without hands-on practice, people are NOT going to learn and retain digital literacy skills.

Free software programs can help us download as well as organize image and video files from our cameras to our computer hard drives. Picassa (www.google.com/picassa) by Google is free and available for both Windows and Apple / Macintosh computers. iPhoto (www.apple.com/ilife/iphoto) is software provided free on every Apple/Macintosh computer which supports media imports as well as organization. The basic steps for importing videos (and photos) in Picassa and iPhoto are similar:

1. Select your camera (after plugging it into your computer)

2. Select videos and photos to import

3. Click Import Selected (or choose to import everything)

   The screenshot below shows these steps in iPhoto '11.

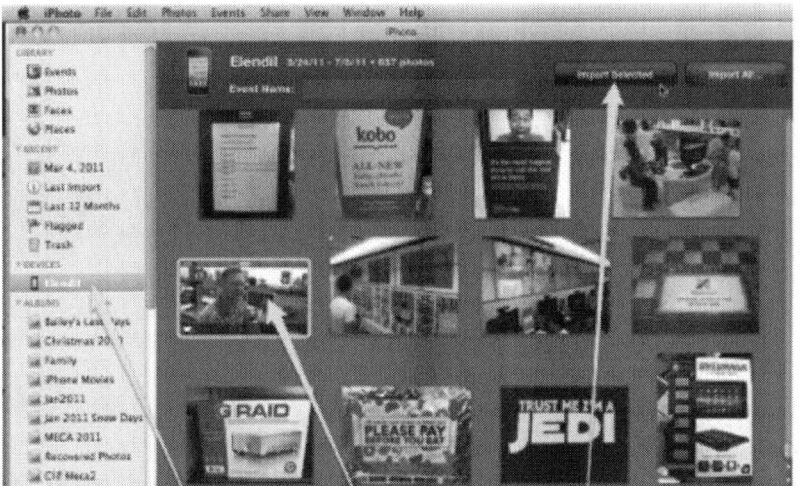

Select your camera, select video & images, & click Import Selected

After importing media to your computer, programs like iPhoto and Picassa will ask if you want to delete the original media files from your camera. This can be an efficient way to keep your camera "clean" of photos and movies you've already imported, but BE SURE you want to delete the file from your camera before choosing this option. Videos and movies can also be directly deleted from your camera later. On Apple computers, the provided utility "Image

Capture" (in Applications) is helpful to use for this. On Windows computers, generally you can browse to the folders containing videos and photos using MY COMPUTER and delete them just like other files on your hard drive.

iPhoto supports direct uploading of video to YouTube, but I also want to share uploading procedures which are applicable for all computer users. Mac users can drag videos and photos out of iPhoto to the desktop or another location on their computers and upload files to YouTube following these instructions.

The key to this process is copying or moving your video file to a location you can identify and find on your computer. The "desktop" folder for your user account on your computer is generally fast to find, and that is why I recommend copying files to the desktop when practicing these steps. The screenshot below shows the location of a movie file I've copied to my desktop, using the "column view" in the Mac OS Finder. This file structure is very similar for all modern operating systems. The actual file is saved on the hard drive, in the Users folder, in my specific User folder, in the Desktop folder, and visible inside it.

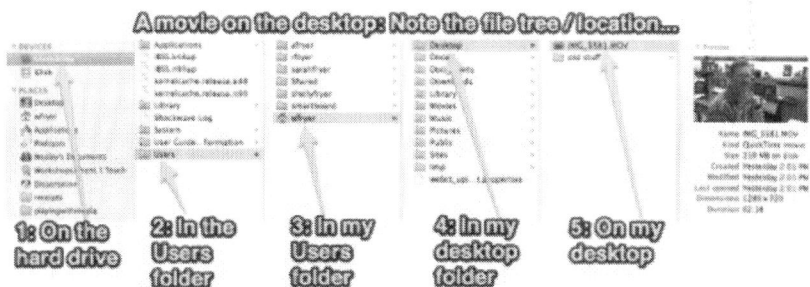

Learning to navigate the file system of your computer is important. Laptop and desktop computers in our schools and homes have file systems which we need to understand and use. Mobile operating systems do not make the file system as accessible and therefore visible to users, which has some advantages. To upload a video using a web browser on a computer, however, we need to understand and be able to use our file systems.

After copying a video file to the desktop, it's time to upload to YouTube. These steps are:

1. Log into www.youtube.com/upload and click the UPLOAD VIDEO button.

2. Select the video you want and click OPEN (in this case, I've navigated to the computer desktop and selected the video)

Click UPLOAD VIDEO and select the video

Once you click OPEN, the video should immediately start uploading to YouTube as long as your computer has an active Internet connection and your local network is configured to permit uploads to YouTube. Fields are provided so you can enter the desired title, description, and "tags" for your video.

The time required to upload your video will vary depending on the size of your video file and the speed of your local Internet connection. In the example above, I was uploading an uncompressed, high definition (720P) video from my iPhone which was 2 minutes and 38 seconds long. This video is just over 200 MB in size.[156]

---

[156] Fryer, W. (2011, July 5). Dell Inspiron duo Convertible Tablet at the Microsoft Store .YouTube - Broadcast Yourself.. Retrieved July 6, 2011, from http://www.youtube.com/watch?v=f_Ib41ZgddU

YouTube provides a <u>thorough series of articles on uploading videos</u>. [157]   I encourage you to check these out for more specific details.

Tagging Videos

Videos and other media content shared online needs to be "tagged" appropriately. Tags are keywords, without spaces, which are attached as "<u>meta</u> information" to a video, photo, or other piece of media content. When uploading a video to YouTube, for example, users are prompted to enter information including the desired title of the video, a description of the video, and "tags" for the video. Tags are very important on YouTube specifically, since the "related videos" which show up in the sidebar of the site are, in part, based on the tags which the owner who uploaded the video specified.

Tags provide a way for media content to be aggregated, or collected. An example was the distributed video project I facilitated for school administrators in Montana. Participants in our two day workshop recorded short video interviews with other school administrators addressing the question, "What does it mean to have 'digital vision' as a school leader in 2011?" Participants uploaded their videos to YouTube and included the <u>tag</u>, "digitalvision2011." By <u>searching YouTube for that tag</u>, I was able to locate participant videos and subsequently download and remix those videos into <u>a single, four minute video</u>. [158]   This is an example of a distributed video project, and is something anyone can facilitate since YouTube

---

[157] Uploading Videos - YouTube Help. (n.d.). Google. Retrieved July 6, 2011, from <u>http://www.google.com/support/youtube/bin/topic.py?topic=16560</u>

[158] Fryer, W. (n.d.). Montana Voices: Digital Vision for Schools 2011 Challenge .YouTube - Broadcast Yourself.. Retrieved July 6, 2011, from <u>http://www.youtube.com/watch?v=8QB64yZBLMc</u>

provides free video hosting for anyone with Internet access worldwide. It may take awhile to get your mind around the possibilities this presents. For more ideas and inspiration, check out Michael Wesch's distributed video project, "Visionsofstudents.org Video Collage."[159] The final project, which is an amazing example of HTML5 video (individual clips are playable as links) is available on visionsofstudents.org.

See Appendix E: iMovie for iPad, for step-by-step instructions. In addition to iMovie, other iOS video editing applications include Splice, ReelDirector, and Vlix. Splice has a free version (with ads) and a 99¢ paid version. ReelDirector is $1.99 and accepts videos created with other apps, where iMovie is "pickier" and seems to only accept video recorded directly on an iOS device. Vlix is free and includes some editing effects options not available in other programs. While the names and features of mobile video editing applications are certain to change in the months ahead. I'm confident the power and utility of these apps is only going to increase.

To stay up to date on mobile videography and other applications for iOS, I recommend subscribing to Tony Vincent's excellent "Learning in Hand" blog (www.learninginhand.com/blog) and following Tony on Twitter @tonyvincent.

Give quick-edit videography a try.

Managing Submitted Student Videos

Since video files are much larger than text, audio or image files, managing videos students submit for assignments and projects can be challenging. In this section, we'll explore several strategies to consider for managing student submitted videos.

---

[159] Wesch, M. (2011, June 19). Visionsofstudents.org Video Collage. Digital Ethnography. Retrieved July 5, 2011, from http://mediatedcultures.net/ksudigg/?p=303

The large file size of videos makes video email attachments a bad idea. While many <u>learning management systems</u> (like <u>Moodle</u> and Blackboard) can technically handle large file attachments and uploads, video files shared on an LMS are not readily sharable on the public web and generally cannot be rated or commented on like videos can be on websites specifically dedicated to video sharing.

Some schools are purchasing sets of flash-based digital camcorders and allowing teachers to check them out like a cart of laptops. If your school has available flash-based camcorders, consider using them with students for a "video scavenger hunt" activity. Feel free to utilize ideas from the <u>video scavenger hunt</u> I conducted with my pre-service education students at the University of Central Oklahoma.[160] Thinking of topics for a video scavenger hunt isn't the most challenging part of this activity, however. Managing the submission of student videos poses a greater challenge.

For older students, YouTube can be an excellent website to host scavenger hunt videos. Teachers should NOT, however, provide students with the direct YouTube login credentials to a created channel. Anyone with those credentials is able to delete, rename, and change any of the videos in the channel. Instead of granting each student this level of "total control" over a shared YouTube channel, it makes more sense to use other methods which function more like a "drop box" for video turn-in. If students have their own YouTube accounts, they can upload video to those accounts and then share the link to their video by emailing it to a class Posterous site. If students dont' have (or you don't necessarily want to require them to create)

---

[160] Fryer, W. (2011, March 30). Flip Video Camera Scavenger Hunt (UCO - Mar 2011). Google Docs. Retrieved July 6, 2011, from <u>https://docs.google.com/document/d/ 1mryV6jenIx0hjE5K0_zjnDMjtnK5vduMv4m3VflpG0U/edit? hl=en_US</u>

personal YouTube accounts,   Pixelpipe.com and Posterous.com are two options for creating a free "video drop box" solution.

Option 1: Pixelpipe

PixelPipe is a website which can upload multiple media types to different "target locations" simultaneously. For example, if you want to upload photos simultaneously to both Facebook and Flickr, PixelPipe can do that for you. For my students, I configured a PixelPipe account to directly upload to the YouTube account and channel I created for our class. (youtube.com/edusandbox) To upload videos, students needed to:

1. Login to PixelPipe with the userid and password I created.
2. Click "Quick Post."
3. Locate their video files individually, just like they would for an email attachment.
4. Enter a title, description, and tags for each video.
5. Click upload.

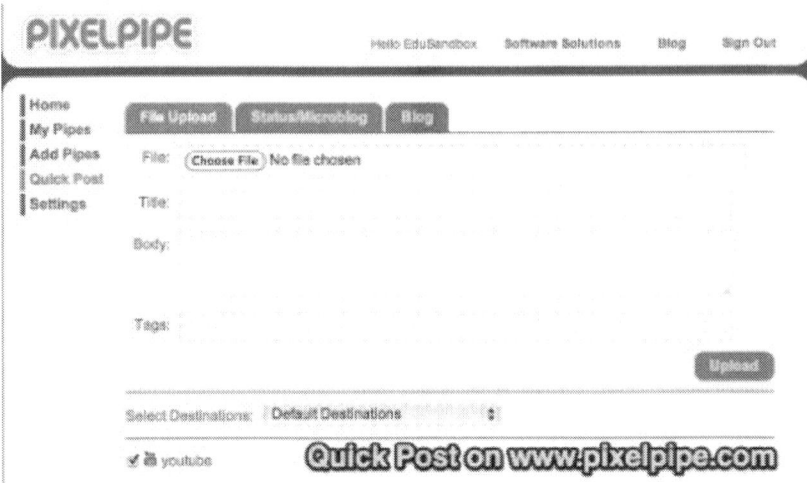

By using PixelPipe, students were able to directly upload videos to YouTube but did not have the YouTube account credentials. This effectively made the site into a "drop box" for a YouTube channel, so videos could be uploaded but not edited or deleted. I was able to make changes, if needed, on the videos after they uploaded to YouTube. I asked students to create blog posts with some of their embedded videos after they uploaded them, and submit their blog post to me (along with information about the students in their group) using a free Google form.

Note that file uploads to PixelPipe require either the use of a laptop/desktop computer and a web browser, OR the free iOS PixelPipe application. PixelPipe mobile apps for iOS and Android have been removed from stores, but will reportedly be re-released.[161]

Option 2: Posterous Blog

---

[161] Wauters, R. (2011, April 25). Pixelpipe Secures $2.3 Million To Help You Share Content With The World. TechCrunch. Retrieved July 6, 2011, from http://techcrunch.com/2011/04/25/pixelpipe-secures-2-3-million-to-help-you-share-content-with-the-world/

A Posterous blog (www.posterous.com) is another option for students to share videos online, but email accounts limit the file sizes of permitted attachments so this can work only for shorter, smaller videos. Keving McGroarty's final presentation video for his fall 2010 class at the Academy of Art University in San Francisco is a good example of how Posterous can be used to share video projects.[162]

Other Video Sharing Options

While students over age 13 technically could upload videos directly to their own YouTube accounts, I would urge caution in assigning students to do this at in middle and high school levels. If your school uses Google Apps and your account administrator has turned on YouTube sharing, uploading there could be a good option. I am not aware of a way students can upload to www.schooltube.com or www.teachertube.com in the "drop box" method I described earlier using PixelPipe. If your school provides a YouTube-clone website, using phpmotion.com, mediascripts.com or another solution, that site can be an ideal place to share videos. Another alternative is a website on Ning.com, but Ning is no longer free and only "Pro" accounts support direct video uploading. Video embedding is supported on other account types.

If you have other ideas and suggestions for managing student video submissions, in addition to those I've outlined here, I'd love to hear about them. I'll continue to post updates on the playingwithmedia.com blog, and share good ideas I learn about from

---

[162] McGroarty, K. (2010, October 21). GR 600 Final Presentation.The Digital Wall by The Academy of Art University in San Francisco. Retrieved July 6, 2011, from http://onlinegrschool.posterous.com/31154549

readers like you with others interested in more efficiently managing student video submissions for assignments and projects.

Video Editing Software

While we all tend to fall victim to "baby duck syndrome" in favoring the computer platforms and software programs we've learned on or used the most, it is beneficial to know about different video editing options on various platforms.[163] One reason for this is diversity. Our students are unlikely to ALL have the same type of computer and operating system at home as we use personally and/or at school. While web-based / cloud-based tools offer the most promise in bridging the gaps between different computer platforms with different operating systems, it seems unlikely we will ever live in a monolithic computing environment where everyone's workstation is the same.

On the Windows side of operating systems, free software tools for still image + audio digital storytelling are PhotoStory3 from Microsoft and the open source program, Audacity.[164] (audacity.sourceforge.net) Some users have found Microsoft's MovieMaker software for WindowsXP unstable on different types of Windows computers. The updated version for Windows7, Windows

---

[163] Baby Duck Syndrome. (n.d.).Wikipedia, the free encyclopedia. Retrieved July 6, 2011, from http://en.wikipedia.org/wiki/Baby_Duck_Syndrome

[164] PhotoStory 3 Software. (n.d.).Microsoft Corporation. Retrieved July 5, 2011, from http://www.microsoft.com/download/en/details.aspx?id=11132

Live MovieMaker, seems to be much-improved although functionality is still quite limited.[165]

Sony Vegas software is a powerful and relatively affordable alternative to MovieMaker on the Windows platform. Michael Wesch is renowned for his YouTube videos (www.youtube.com/user/mwesch) which have received over 20 million combined views worldwide as of this writing. Sony Vegas is the program he uses and recommends to other Windows users. Vegas software is offered as a product family (www.sonycreativesoftware.com/vegassoftware) and the entry-level software can be purchased for $45.

iMovie software (www.apple.com/ilife/imovie) has been significantly changed and updated since it was introduced in the late 1990s. A major factor in this update is the ability to support realtime editing (versus time-delayed rendering in previous versions) made possible because of faster computing power as well as flash-based camcorders. From 2003 through June 2011, Apple offered a simplified version of it's Final Cut Pro video editing software called Final Cut Express.[166] While some other video editing software programs exist for Mac users, iMovie and Final Cut Pro (now available via Mac App Store for $299, a dramatically reduced price) are the only ones I'd recommend for video production.[167]

---

[165] Fryer, W. (2010, January 9). Getting Creative with Windows Live Movie Maker on a Netbook. Moving at the Speed of Creativity. Retrieved July 6, 2011, from http://www.speedofcreativity.org/2010/01/09/getting-creative-with-windows-live-movie-maker-on-a-netbook/

[166] Final Cut Express. (n.d.).Wikipedia, the free encyclopedia. Retrieved July 6, 2011, from http://en.wikipedia.org/wiki/Final_Cut_Express

[167] Final Cut Pro X - A revolution in creative editing. (n.d.). Apple. Retrieved July 6, 2011, from http://www.apple.com/finalcutpro

Advanced Stuff: CODECs and Video Players

Computers ship with default video and media playback software which their operating system creators hope you'll use exclusively. A variety of different video CODECs (the software used to decode digitized video) are used on different websites, however, so it's a good idea to install several as well as different types of video "player" software to ensure you can play back different videos.[168]

VLC Media Player (www.videolan.org/vlc) is a free, open source video playback software program compatible with Windows, Macintosh and Linux computer systems. Open video formats "matter" because they are not owned and controlled by corporations and licensing fees are not required to encode or decode videos in these formats. Many popular media formats, including Flash, MP3 and MPEG4, are proprietary formats. Users of proprietary media formats are generally not changed fees, but content creators who encode into them are charged fees. We live in a multi-platform, diverse ecosystem of computer operating systems which are interoperable in many ways thanks to the Internet. Open standards and formats are very important for multiple reasons, including the cause of open access to information around the globe. By using and encouraging others to use open media players like VLC which support open CODECs, we can advance the non-commercial goal of supporting open media standards.

Apple / Macintosh computers ship with QuickTime software as the default media player application. QuickTime is available for Windows computers as well (www.apple.com/quicktime/download.) I recommend enhancing the playback CODEC options of

---

[168] Codec. (n.d.). Wikipedia, the free encyclopedia. Retrieved July 5, 2011, from http://en.wikipedia.org/wiki/Codec

QuickTime on Apple computers by installing Perian (perian.org) and Microsoft's "Windows Media Components for QuickTime."[169]

On the Windows side of operating systems, the Combined Community Codec Pack (CCCP) is a collection of different media CODECS which can be downloaded and installed together.[170] By installing Apple QuickTime and the CCCP, a Windows computer can play back most media types and video formats.

The main video CODEC format I've been unable to play on different operating systems is the Windows Media Video file format created by Microsoft's free PhotoStory3 program.[171] Regardless of the CODECs I've downloaded and tried, I have been unable to play exported PhotoStory3 videos on Apple / Macintosh computers. The best workaround to this seems to be uploading the videos to Ning and watching them as converted Flash videos on Apple computers. (Not iOS devices, however.)

Closing Thoughts

Video is a major communication medium in our information landscape today. As educators, we need to possess strong senses of digital literacy in both the use of and creation of video. I hope the ideas shared in this chapter have given you more ideas about ways to incorporate video effectively within your lessons as well as your

---

[169] Windows Media Components for QuickTime . (n.d.).Microsoft . Retrieved July 5, 2011, from http://windows.microsoft.com/en-US/windows/products/windows-media-player/wmcomponents

[170] CCCP. (n.d.). Combined Community Codec Pack. Retrieved July 5, 2011, from http://www.cccp-project.net

[171] PhotoStory 3 Software. (n.d.).Microsoft Corporation. Retrieved July 5, 2011, from http://www.microsoft.com/download/en/details.aspx?id=11132

assignments for students. Take time to play with video, creating and sharing it using some of the tools and websites described in this chapter. If you don't play with video, you won't learn how to leverage it more effectively for learning with your students. As you proceed on your journey of learning with video, please remember to share your ideas with others along the way!

7- Show & Tell

Sarah Fryer teaching about VoiceThread during the MACE 2011 Keynote [172]

It's a myth students stop enjoying and needing "show and tell" after kindergarten or first grade. We need to provide more opportunities for "digital show and tell" inside and outside our classrooms as we play with media and ask our students to "show what they know" using media. These show and tell opportunities can take multiple forms, but all can accomplish similar objectives:

---

[172] Fryer, W. (2011, March 3). Sarah teaching about VoiceThread during the MACE 2011 Keynote. Welcome to Flickr - Photo Sharing. Retrieved July 6, 2011, from http://www.flickr.com/photos/wfryer/5535100058/in/set-72157626161376669/

1. Celebrate, recognize and "edify" students for their learning and hard work

2. Provide parents and other caregivers with greater opportunities to peer through "digital windows" into their child's perceptions, skills, ideas and achievements

3. Visibly document evidences of learning for students, parents, and the school community

4. Create digital artifacts which can become elements in students' digital portfolios

Digital show and tell can also play an important role in shaping the perceptions of parents and other taxpayers in your community about your school. The "Nebraska Loves Public Schools" project (nelovesps.org) is the best example I've seen to date of a statewide initiative specifically seeking to improve taxpayer perceptions of teachers, teaching, and public schools through the a digital media campaign.

Nebraska Loves Public Schools [173]

Organizers for NElovesPS conducted research about voters in Nebraska, and found over 70% do not have a personal, direct connection to anyone currently learning Nebraska Public Schools.[174] The perceptions of this voting majority were (and largely still are) being driven by press coverage in mainstream media channels. Sponsors at the Omaha-based Sherwood Foundation (www.sherwoodfoundation.org) recognized the power and potential for web-based video to change perceptions and be shared virally

---

[173] Welcome to NELovesPS.org. (n.d.). Nebraska Loves Public Schools. Retrieved July 9, 2011, from http://nelovesps.org

[174] Nellson, Sally. Interview by author. Phone interview. Oklahoma City, OK and Omaha, NE, June 7, 2011.

through social networks like Facebook and Twitter. This ongoing project is an example of professional videography. Video projects created using "quick-edit" and "no-edit" techniques described in the preceding chapters are NOT going to rival the quality of NElovesPS videos. The project demonstrates the potential for school advocates to leverage the power of digital video as well as social media to effect educational change. Learners in all our schools (not just in Nebraska) need to be "telling the story" of the good learning taking place inside and outside our classrooms. I hope the ideas in this chapter inspire and empower you to become a local storychaser (www.storychasers.org) of superb learning in your community. Digital show and tell can have many purposes, but one of the most important is letting our community constituents know the value of our public schools as we amplify outstanding examples of great learning using technology.

Showcasing Digital Work Online

"The Digital Wall" (onlinegrschool.posterous.com) is an online showcase of student work from the School Of Graphic Design in the San Francisco-based Academy Of Art University. Images of student work are shared as separate files embedded in posts, and as longer documents embedded with the website Scribd.com.

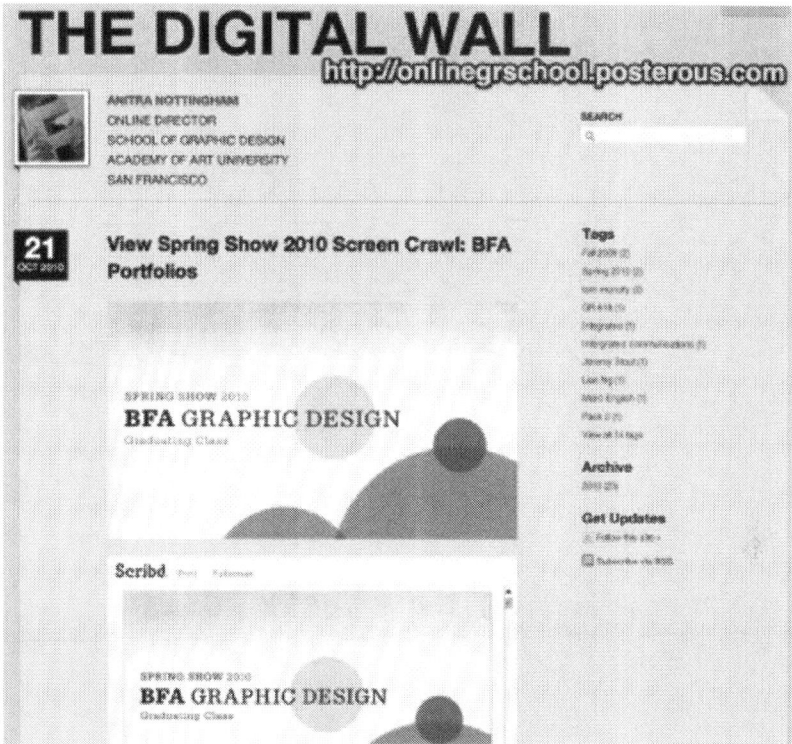

The Digital Wall [175]

Many different websites are used by educators and students to showcase learning. This example uses the free website, Posterous.com. As discussed in preceding chapters on "Digital Text" and "Images," Posterous sites can be used to efficiently share a variety of rich media online. By emailing links to other websites and including rich media files as email attachments, students and teachers can create websites like this. Posterous site owners can moderate and publish submissions from others online.

---

[175] The Digital Wall - All the best online student work. (2010). Posterous.com. Retrieved July 24, 2011, from http:// onlinegrschool.posterous.com

Sites like these can become a media channel of aggregated content for parents, students, and other interested people to visit. Web feeds (RSS feeds) are created by blog sites including Posterous. Web feeds permit people to SUBSCRIBE to these channels of content and add them to their "digital dashboards" for media reading and consumption. Flipboard for iPad (www.flipboard.com) is one example. Publishing media content on a site which supports web feeds is far more powerful than simply posting content on a static website. As more people shift to digital consumption of news and information, these websites will grow in their utility as well as reach.

Other "quick-share" websites in addition to Posterous can be used to showcase student work. Rock Our World (www.rockourworld.org) is an international, collaborative education project organized by California teacher Carol Anne McGuire. Carol uses a free Tumblr blog (rockourworld-official.tumblr.com) to publish student project videos. These posts include uploaded video files, links to videos shared on other websites like YouTube, and other text posts including hyperlinks.

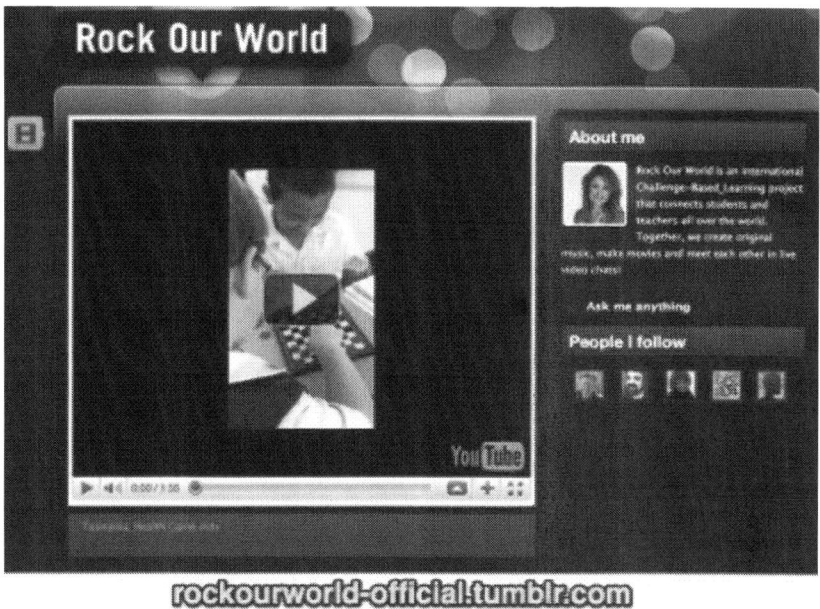

rockourworld-official.tumblr.com

Student Digital Portfolios

There are many ways we can "show what we know" as well as what we can do. While standardized tests and multiple choice assessments can offer efficient ways to test student knowledge, they generally cannot assess higher order thinking skills, creativity, and domains like digital literacy. Digital media offers almost limitless possibilities for demonstrating knowledge and skills. As you play with media and gain greater digital agency communicating with text, images, audio and video, you can and should help your students create "digital knowledge artifacts" which can become elements in their online portfolios. As educators, we can and should aggregate our own professional portfolios to demonstrate our educational philosophies and teaching skills.

Students as well as teachers should create a wide variety of digital artifacts using text, images, audio and video, and aggregate links to those online products using a wiki. Give preference to web-based tools which save media "in the cloud," because these sites generally provide direct links you can use and often "embed" within your own digital portfolio website. A wide variety of wiki tools are available. The two free options I recommend are:

1. WikiSpaces for Educators (www.wikispaces.com/content/for/teachers)

2. Google Sites (sites.google.com)

WikiSpaces, in my experience, permits a greater number of "embed code" types on its pages. Google Sites, however, is excellent and supports free sub-domain mapping of sites you create to domains you own. This is one of the reasons I use Google Sites for my own professional wiki, wiki.wesfryer.com. While it is certainly not necessary to "map" a wiki site to a custom domain, it does make the site appear more professional as well as easier to share with others as a shorter website address. Of course, that depends on how short your domain name is.

Here are some examples of professional educator digital portfolios, created with different kinds of wiki tools.

1. Rachel Boyd: Created with WikiSpaces. Rachel is a primary years teacher and school administrator in Auckland, New Zealand.[176]

2. Shannon Miller: Created with Google Sites. Shannon is a Library Media Specialist at Van Meter School, Iowa. Shannon

---

[176] Boyd, R. (2007). Rachel Boyd's Professional Portfolio. Wikispaces.com. Retrieved July 8, 2011, from http://rachelboyd.wikispaces.com

has used a DNS configuration so her site is also accessible from shannonmmiller.com.[177]

3. Andrea Smith: Created with Weebly. Andrea is an international teacher in Asia.[178]

Each of these professional educator portfolio examples are published on the OPEN versus the CLOSED web. This means a userid and password are not required to access these sites. Open web publishing is essential to take ownership and control over your "digital footprint," the collection of websites which come up in Internet searches for your name. While websites in the United States which include personal profile information are officially restricted to students over age 13, there is not a definitive rule on WHEN students should publish online using their own name. Kevin Honeycutt (www.kevinhoneycutt.com) suggests students can publish at younger ages under an alias, and then "claim" their different online works by linking them from an aggregated digital portfolio when they are older and decide to do so with their parents.

Senior students at Nokomis High School in Newport, Maine, are presented with their own domain name when they graduate.[179] Colby Ratzlaff presented the keynote address in the "Student

[177] Miller, S. M. (2009). Professional Portfolio of Shannon McClintock Miller. Google Sites. Retrieved July 8, 2011, from http://sites.google.com/site/unishannonmillerportfolio/home

[178] Smith, A. (2010). Andrea Smith's Portfolio.Weebly.com. Retrieved July 9, 2011, from http://andreasmith.weebly.com

[179] Kelly, Kern. Director of Education Technology in central Maine at Regional School Unit #19. Interview by author. Personal interview. Boulder, CO, August 5, 2009.

Voices" strand of the 2010 K-12 Online Conference.[180] Colby's digital portfolio (sites.google.com/site/colbyratz/) showcases his original art and links to his accepted contributions in the Google 3D Warehouse, created with Google Sketchup. These kinds of open web digital portfolios are, in my view, the best kind of digital portfolios for our students in school to create. Open web, free digital portfolios can document students' learning journeys over time and become professional tools to complement resumes and other job application materials. Web services like Google Profiles (profiles.google.com) and claimid.com can also be used to stake out a "digital claim" online and proactively manage your digital footprint.

Many colleges of education as well as some K-12 schools have mandated digital portfolios for students as well as teachers. "Online Student Portfolios: What Tools Are Best?" highlights some of those

---

[180] Ratzlaff, C. (2010, October 18). STUDENT VOICES KEYNOTE: The Life Practice Model: a real life example. K12 Online Conference 2010 . Retrieved July 9, 2011, from http://k12onlineconference.org/?p=642

platforms and their relative benefits. Schools and individuals approach digital / electronic portfolios in two general ways:

1. Centralized, standardized ePortfolio Solutions
2. Distributed, User Customized ePortfolios

Many colleges of education have favored the first of these options: centralized, standardized solutions. Commercial ePortfolio vendors like TaskStream (www.taskstream.com) and PassPort (passport.org) are examples of standardized, fee-based ePortfolio systems used by colleges for pre-service students. Universities often pass on the costs for these ePortfolio solutions to students, requiring them to subscribe to the service as a part of their degree and/or certificate programs. While these commercial ePortfolio systems can help colleges demonstrate student completion of program requirements for accreditation bodies like NCATE (The National Council for Accreditation of Teacher Education) they are rarely sustained by students following graduation to maintain professional ePortfolios. The annual subscription costs of these services, although not substantial, are high enough that most students decide not to pay them when they complete their university education programs. [181]

Open source ePortfolio systems are utilized by some K-12 schools, and generally costs are borne by schools / institutions rather than individual students utilizing them. Mahara (mahara.org) is an open source electronic portfolio content management system developed in New Zealand. Foliospaces (www.foliospaces.com) is a commercial ePortfolio system with a "freemium" model, where some storage and services are provided for free but additional features require payment. A custom implementation of the open source

---

[181] Owens-Delong, Dana. Director of Technology for the College of Education at the University of Central Oklahoma. Interview by author. Personal interview. Edmond, OK, February 16, 2011.

learning managment system, Sakai (sakaiproject.org,) is being utilized for teacher and student digital portfolios among a collaborative group of schools in the northeastern United States (sau53.sakaizone.org.) New Tech Network schools (www.newtechnetwork.org) has utilized a learning management system which hybridizes Moodle, Google Docs, and Drupal.[182]

Centralized ePortfolio management systems like those described here can offer advantages as well as costs to both schools and individual students. In the years ahead it is virtually certain (pun intended) school leaders will continue to explore a wide variety of digital portfolio options. Whatever ePortfolio "system" your school chooses to embrace and support, or not support, the creation of linkable, web-based digital portfolio artifacts online can be integrated into those systems via hyperlinks as well as embed codes. Since some websites will come and go, downloading offline versions of projects and/or creating screencasts of projects which are cross-posted to other websites can serve as "digital insurance" for portfolio elements. Consider these kinds of backup steps for digital artifacts which are particularly exemplary and you (or your students) do not want to lose under any circumstances.

Helen Barrett's website (electronicportfolios.com) is a good resource for examples and resources related to digital portfolios. Digital Portfolios Made Easy (www.dpme.org) by Leigh Zeitz and Andrew Krumm is also a good resource site. Both Helen and Leigh recommend using Google Sites as a free, flexible platform for creating electronic portfolios designed to not only reflect personal skills and passions, but also demonstrate mastery of specific standards and program requirements specific to your school, state, or accrediting organization.

---

[182] Walsh, C. (2009). Moogpal in Action. K12 Online Conference. Retrieved July 9, 2011, from http://k12onlineconference.org/?p=471

Updating Facebook

Facebook has become an important communications platform in our digitally connected society. I do not advocate that educators use Facebook as a "learning management system" to replace a Moodle, Sakai, BlackBoard/WebCT, Desire2Learn or other formal learning portal for course materials, but I DO advocate the use of Facebook to communicate more effectively with parents as well as students. A Facebook page can become an important communication tool for individual classroom teachers, as well as school / school district administrators and public relations officials.

To understand why Facebook is so important to use today as a modern educator, let's consider a few statistics as well as an analogy. In 2010, for the first time, Facebook.com had more global pageviews worldwide than Google.[183] If Facebook were a country, in June 2011 it would have been the third largest on our planet.[184] More and more of our students and parents in the United States are using Facebook as a platform for accessing and sharing information. It can be hard to get parents to visit your school website on a regular basis. It's easier to communicate with them, "where they live," on Facebook.

An analogy of a "personal radar screen" can be helpful to understand why Facebook is such an important communications platform today. Individuals involved in air traffic control, like the

---

[183] Sherman, A. (n.d.). Facebook passes Google as most visited US site. Featured Articles From Boston.com. Retrieved June 3, 2011, from http://articles.boston.com/2011-01-01/business/29337357_1_facebook-google-social-networking

[184] Tsukayama, H. (n.d.). Facebook poised to hit 700 million users. The Washington Post: National, World & D.C. Area News and Headlines - The Washington Post. Retrieved June 4, 2011, from http://www.washingtonpost.com/blogs/faster-forward/post/facebook-poised-to-hit-700-million-users/2011/05/31/AGp7FQFH_blog.html

military member pictured in the image below, constantly watch radar screens to learn new information.

A sergeant monitors a radar screen by expertinfantry [185]

[185] expertinfantry. (2011, February 21). A sergeant monitors a radar screen. Flickr - Photo Sharing. Retrieved July 16, 2011, from http://www.flickr.com/photos/expertinfantry/5467649200/

Facebook is a significant part of the 'personal information radar screens' of many people today. Since Facebook is increasingly "where people live" in a virtual sense, it makes a great deal of logical sense for educators to share information there. The way to do this is by creating a Facebook page.

To create a Facebook "fan page" others can follow:

1. Create a Facebook account, if you have not already.

2. Lot into your Facebook account in a web browser.

3. Visit www.facebook.com/pages/create.php to create a page. At this writing, Facebook will prompt you with six category choices to create your page.

If you'd like to create a formal, "Teacher page" to share information with parents of your students as well as the students directly, choose the category "Artist, Band or Public Figure" and choose "Teacher" from the drop down menu of available options. After agreeing to Facebook's terms of use, you can create and customize your page.

Facebook pages can be used for school clubs, sports teams, school committees, or almost any other organization related to education you can imagine. While you (and others who you grant permission to update your Facebook page, if desired) can directly update the "news feed" on your page using a web browser logged into Facebook.com, it can be handy (as well as efficient) to configure your Facebook page to automatically update whenever a new post is shared on a blog site related to your organization. This way, people can "like" or follow your Facebook page and receive all your updates right within their Facebook news feed, even when you are posting to your class, personal or organizational blog and not directly updating Facebook.

Words of Caution Regarding Facebook Pages

Be aware of the different "permissions" which can be set for a Facebook page. As a teacher, you may want to uncheck the options to allow users to "write or post content on the wall" of your page, add photos and add videos. If you DO allow these permissions for users, be SURE to frequently check your Facebook page and moderate submissions of content you receive there. A significant part of the inherent power and draw of social media websites like Facebook is their potential for interactivity, and "disallowing" permission for your parents as well as students to interact/post on your Facebook page may be a bad thing for your communication with them. On the other hand, it can be disastrous if offensive or demeaning content gets posted to YOUR Facebook page and others see it. You need to consider your options and decide what settings make the most sense. The example screenshot below shows permission settings for a FaceBook Teacher Page with user posting abilities disabled:

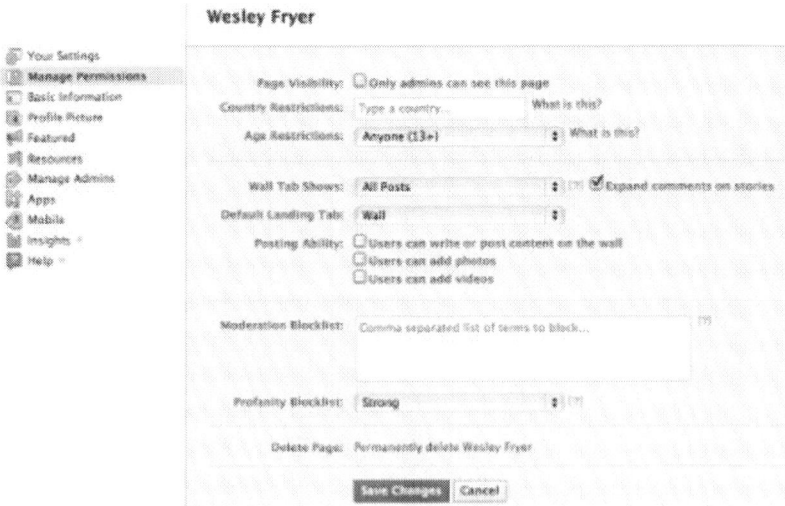

If you DO choose to enable user posting on a Facebook page, I recommend setting the "Profanity Blocklist" to the "Strong" setting, and also designating multiple, responsible individuals to help you monitor and moderate content on the page. Facebook provides a Help page explaining how to "proactively moderate content posted on my Page."[186]

Twitterfeed.com is a free website which provides a mechanism for auto-posting content from a blog or other website to a Facebook page you've created. A five minute screencast available on Screenr and on YouTube demonstrates how to use Twitterfeed to connect a Facebook page to a blog.[187]

Canadian educator Dean Shareski alerted me to the capabilities of Twitterfeed.com.[188] Dean collaborated with me to design the first "Playing with Media: simple ideas for powerful sharing" workshop. If you do not already, be sure to follow Dean on Twitter @shareski and subscribe to his blog, "Ideas and Thoughts of an EdTech."[189]

---

[186] How can I proactively moderate content posted on my Page? (n.d.). Facebook Help. Retrieved June 4, 2011, from http://www.facebook.com/help/new/?faq=19793

[187] Fryer, W. (2010, April 10). How to automatically publish blog posts to a Facebook page. YouTube - Broadcast Yourself. Retrieved July 21, 2011, from http://www.youtube.com/watch?v=iilp73J11OQ

[188] Sprankle, B. (2011, January 7). Seedlings @ Bit By Bit Podcast: Show 102. Bit by Bit: Weblog of Bob Sprankle. Retrieved June 4, 2011, from http://bobsprankle.com/bitbybit_wordpress/?p=2828

[189] Shareski, D. (2005). Blog of Dean Shareski. Ideas and Thoughts of an EdTech. Retrieved July 9, 2011, from http://ideasandthoughts.org

Sharing Celebrations

We live in an increasingly digital information environment awash in media. Your students may create hundreds of digital artifacts using text, images, audio and video during the academic year, but parents and others may not pay attention to these learning products unless you work to create a sense of immediacy and urgency with scheduled celebration sharing events. Consider hosting "digital open house" events in your classroom or for your school at least once per term. The digital storytelling contest celebration events (modeled after the Academy Awards) hosted by Mabry Middle School in Cobb County, Georgia, under the leadership of former principal Tim Tyson, are an exemplar for these kinds of events.[190] Film Festivals organized by Marco Torres and his SFETT student team in the 1990s at San Fernando High School, in Los Angeles, California, are another "shining star" example.[191] Both of these examples were events which brought in many members of each community, who came to see "the digital work" of students and family members.

School PTA/PTO groups typically have the highest parent attendance at meetings when students perform to show off their skills. Media sharing nights have the benefit of not requiring "live performances" of students: Everyone can relax and enjoy the event, since "performances" were already recorded in advance.

---

[190] Fryer, W. (2007, June 28). Podcast164: Dr. Tim Tyson's NECC 2007 Closing Keynote.Moving at the Speed of Creativity. Retrieved July 9, 2011, from http://www.speedofcreativity.org/2007/06/28/podcast164-dr-tim-tysons-necc-2007-closing-keynote/

[191] EduTopia Staff. (2002). Multimedia Serves Youths' Desire to Express Themselves. Edutopia: K-12 Education & Learning Innovations with Proven Strategies that Work. Retrieved July 9, 2011, from http://www.edutopia.org/san-fernando-education-technology-multimedia

When students share video projects and other media creations with a live audience in your classroom or school auditorium, consider asking them to share some of the "backstory" about their project. What did they find most challenging? What was surprising about their research? What would they change if they could about their project? A student "master of ceremonies" can facilitate these questions, which can add a great deal of insight into the work as well as learning which went into student projects.

Please share your successes and learning experiences as you organize media sharing events for your classroom and school. Digital sharing can be wonderful and transformational, allowing people to read, hear, and watch student learning in action at times and in places where it would not otherwise be possible without technology. Face-to-face celebration and sharing events can be even more powerful, however, especially as we celebrate and recognize the hard work of students in front of peers as well as family members.

Referenced Videos & Screencasts

Seventeen videos and screencasts are referenced in this book. If you are reading the multimedia EPUB version, these videos are embedded in your eBook. If you are reading the paper-based / analog version or the standard eBook version, however, you'll need to use hyperlinks to view these videos. Most of my videos and screencasts are published on the following channels, to which you are welcome as a free subscriber.

www.youtube.com/wfryer

vimeo.com/wfryer

www.screenr.com/user/wfryer

These videos are also embedded and linked from the PlayingWithMedia.com website.

Chapter 2 - Digital Text

Fryer, W. (2011). Set up a Moderated Class Blog on Posterous. YouTube - Broadcast Yourself. Retrieved June 23, 2011, from http://www.youtube.com/watch?v=Pf17216KpL0

Chapter 3 - Audio

Fryer, R. (2009, July 14). USS Arizona Impressions (AudioBoo by 5 year old Rachel). YouTube - Broadcast Yourself. Retrieved June 24, 2011, from http://www.youtube.com/watch?v=vfT40tC2Hcs

How to record a phone interview as a phonecast using iPadio.com. (n.d.). Screenr | Instant screencasts: Just click record. Retrieved June 2, 2011, from http://www.screenr.com/rA5. Also available on www.youtube.com/watch?v=Ds5jTOgD_JY

Chapter 5 - Images

Fryer, W. (2011, February 2). How to find and use Creative Commons images in blog posts - YouTube . YouTube - Broadcast Yourself. . Retrieved July 21, 2011, from http://www.youtube.com/watch?v=ONIagUKG7Vs

Fryer, S. (2010, March 24). A VoiceThread about Helen Keller. YouTube - Broadcast Yourself. Retrieved July 21, 2011, from http://www.youtube.com/watch?v=I3vYmKg3aww

Fryer, W. (2011, January 28). How to create a new educator account on VoiceThread.com. YouTube - Broadcast Yourself. Retrieved July 21, 2011, from http://www.youtube.com/watch?v=3KZOxlgKIbU

Fryer, W. (2010, January 28). Part 1 of 3: Creating a VoiceThread (images). YouTube - Broadcast Yourself. . Retrieved July 21, 2011, from http://www.youtube.com/watch?v=7cyuGg1ORPc

Fryer, W. (2010, January 28). Part 2 of 3: Creating a VoiceThread (comments). YouTube - Broadcast Yourself. Retrieved July 21, 2011, from http://www.youtube.com/watch?v=rzwR9o9dOew

Fryer, W. (2010, January 28). Part 3 of 3: Creating a VoiceThread (sharing). YouTube - Broadcast Yourself. Retrieved July 21, 2011, from http://www.youtube.com/watch?v=Hf1SZ0-duEA

Chapter 6 - Video

Fryer, S., & Fryer, R. (2011, March 15). The beach (a narrated slideshow created with SonicPics). YouTube - Broadcast Yourself. Retrieved July 12, 2011, from http://www.youtube.com/watch?v=9W3DjgWJtB0

Fryer, W. (2010, November 13). Using StoryKit, Storyrobe and Sonic Pics on an iOS Device. YouTube - Broadcast Yourself. Retrieved July 6, 2011, from http://www.youtube.com/watch?v=PKSzIiQ8Xbc

Fryer, R. (2010, November 3). The Importance of Art Class at School and Creativity. YouTube - Broadcast Yourself. Retrieved July 12, 2011, from http://www.youtube.com/watch?v=WkZV-QwpweM

Hokanson, K., & Fryer, W. (2011, June 28). Copyright Advice for Teachers from Kristin Hokanson. YouTube - Broadcast Yourself. Retrieved July 14, 2011, from http://www.youtube.com/watch?v=g4rTfZOX-IM

Fryer, W. (2011, January 5). How to turn on YouTube video comment moderation. YouTube - Broadcast Yourself.. Retrieved July 12, 2011, from http://www.youtube.com/watch?v=l-KHBleJEhg

Fryer, W. (2011, January 14). MySpace Suicide Prevention. YouTube - Broadcast Yourself.. Retrieved July 11, 2011, from http://www.youtube.com/watch?v=sdsdWn2w194

Chapter 7 - Show and Tell

Fryer, W. (2010, April 10). How to automatically publish blog posts to a Facebook page. YouTube - Broadcast Yourself. . Retrieved July 21, 2011, from http://www.youtube.com/watch?v=iilp73J11OQ

Appendix C: Audio Software & Lecturecasts

Fryer, W. (2010, December 8). How I use a mobile audio recorder and free software (Switch and Podcast Generator) to publish audio lecturecasts. Screenr | Instant screencasts: Just click record . Retrieved July 21, 2011, from http://www.screenr.com/t6L. Also available on www.youtube.com/watch?v=M53NaUO9aFg

More Resources

In addition to the resources already included in this book, I recommend the following websites, organizations, and projects for additional ideas related to "playing with media."

The FREE K-12 Online Conference

K12 Online Conference 2010

CULTIVATING THE FUTURE

K12 online 2010

k12onlineconference.org

Since 2006, the FREE K-12 Online Conference (www.k12onlineconference.org) has offered world-class opportunities for educators around the world to share innovative ideas and best practices related to the creative integration of technology in the classroom. Over forty presentations have been shared EACH YEAR, and remain archived online.

http://k12onlineconference.org/docs/k12online06-agenda.html

http://k12onlineconference.org/docs/k12online2007schedule.html

http://k12onlineconference.org/docs/k12online2008schedule.html

http://wiki.k12onlineconference.org/home/for-participants/
2009-schedule

http://wiki.k12onlineconference.org/home/for-participants/
2010-schedule

These presentations are also available in downloadable, iOS-compatible video as well as audio-only podcast versions.[192] I encourage you to not only utilize presentation content from K-12 Online, but also share the workshop as an outstanding source of professional development curriculum with other teachers at your school.

EduTopia

EduTopia (www.edutopia.org) is the educational outreach website of the George Lucas Educational Foundation (GLEF). GLEF's vision is:

> ... of a new world of learning, a place where
> students and parents, teachers and
> administrators, policy makers and the people
> they serve are all empowered to change

---

[192] K-12 Online Conference Web feeds. (n.d.). K12 Online Conference. Retrieved July 11, 2011, from http://k12onlineconference.org/?page_id=147

education for the better; a place where schools provide rigorous project-based learning, social-emotional learning, and access to new technology; a place where innovation is the rule, not the exception; a place where students become lifelong learners and develop 21st-century skills, especially in information literacy so they can:

- find, assess, and use information effectively and creatively

- work cooperatively and constructively with others

- use their strengths and talents to become empowered, productive citizens in our democratic society and the world at large.

EduTopia videos (www.edutopia.org/video), resources on project-based learning (www.edutopia.org/project-based-learning) and the Digital Generation Project (www.edutopia.org/digital-generation) are particularly useful sections of their website filled with ideas to share with both teachers and students. I have enjoyed using "youth profile" videos of students included in the Digital Generation Project with my pre-service education students to catalyze conversations about technology's role in learning and the capabilities of young people to engage in complex communication activities using digital tools.

The Buck Institute for Education

The Buck Institute for Education (www.bie.org) is a fantastic organization promoting project-based learning (PBL) in classrooms and schools. They offer a great collection of PBL tools (www.bie.org/tools) for educators, including free as well as commercial versions. The Buck Institute media library includes videos defining and explaining PBL (www.bie.org/videos/cat/what_is_pbl), example PBL project videos (www.bie.org/videos/cat/example_projects), and PBL "how to" videos (www.bie.org/videos/cat/how_to_do_pbl).

Story Chasers Inc.

Story Chasers Inc. (www.storychasers.org) is an Oklahoma-based nonprofit for which I serve as executive director. The work of Storychasers started in 2007 as a statewide oral history and digital storytelling project for the Oklahoma state centennial. Since that time, over 1000 teachers in Oklahoma, Kansas and Texas have participated in multi-day workshops focused on digital storytelling. Storychasers provides workshops and moderated, online learning communities empowering learners to become digital witnesses, archiving local oral history and sharing that history safely on the global stage of the Internet. Project videos created by teachers and students are available on the following Ning learning communities, moderated by Storychaser facilitators:

1. Oklahoma: lc.celebrateoklahoma.us./video

2. Kansas: celebratekansas.ning.com/video

3. Texas: celebratetexas.ning.com/video

Storychasers offers a variety of free resources on its wiki (info.storychasers.org) of interest to media creators and digital storytellers, including:

1. Image resources (info.storychasers.org/home/resources/images)

2. Audio and Music resources (info.storychasers.org/home/resources/audio)

3. Copyright and Fair Use resources (info.storychasers.org/home/resources/copyright)

4. Software resources (info.storychasers.org/home/resources/software)

5. Workshop handouts (info.storychasers.org/home/resources/handouts)

Although Storychasers works primarily (as of this writing) in Oklahoma, Kansas and Texas, certified facilitators are available to lead workshops anywhere. More information about hosting a Storychasers' workshop is available on the website FAQ.[193]

---

[193] Frequently Asked Questions (FAQs). (n.d.). StoryChasers. Retrieved July 11, 2011, from http://storychasers.org/faq/

Appendix A: Balanced Content Filtering in Schools

It is important to address the issue of content filtering in our schools. US law requires all schools and libraries (both public and private) receiving federal E-Rate funds have a policy for blocking access to objectionable Internet content and enforce that policy. This is part of the Children's Internet Project Act, or CIPA law. I am an advocate for balanced content filtering in schools as well as libraries.[194] There are good reasons to block access to pornography and other types of content in our schools, and limited censorship policies in our US schools are not only required by the law but also beneficial for the children who learn there. Internet censorship is out of control in many US schools today, however, and has become a major obstacle we need to address effectively to develop the media literacy skills highlighted in this book.

Many schools in the United States currently "overblock" Internet websites far beyond the levels required by US law. In 2007 after visiting China for the first time, I conducted an informal comparison between sites which were blocked in my hotel by the Chinese government and those blocked in an Oklahoma school district I visited for an E-Rate presentation on behalf of AT&T later the same month. Of the fifteen sites I included in my comparative study, five were blocked in China. Nine were blocked in the Norman Public Schools.

---

[194] Fryer, W. (n.d.). Home. Balanced Filtering in Schools. Retrieved July 2, 2011, from http://balancedfiltering.org/

231

Website	Accessible in China?	Accessible in my U.S. school district location today?
WikiPedia	[URL blocked]	Yes
My blog	Yes	Yes
WordPress.com (view only)	Yes	Yes
WordPress.com (edit/dashboard)	[URL blocked]	Yes
EduBlogs	[URL blocked]	Yes
PBwiki sites (like my workshop curriculum)	[URL blocked]	Yes
WikiSpaces sites	Yes	[URL blocked]
Flickr	[URL blocked] (can access the site but all images are blocked)	[URL blocked]
Technorati	Yes	[URL blocked]
Yahoo Mail	Yes	[URL blocked]
Blogger.com sites	not sure	[URL blocked]
proxify.com (used to bypass content filters)	Yes	[URL blocked]
Access Flickr FireFox Plug-In	Yes (can download and it works)	[URL blocked] (can't download, if already installed it does NOT work)
Google Notebook	Yes	[URL blocked]
Google Documents	Yes	[URL blocked]
# Blocked Domains:	5	9

Content Filtering in Communist China versus an Oklahoma School by
Wesley Fryer [195]

[195] Fryer, W. (2007, September 27). Content filtering in Communist China versus an Oklahoma school. Moving at the Speed of Creativity. Retrieved July 2, 2011, from http://www.speedofcreativity.org/2007/09/25/content-filtering-in-communist-china-versus-an-oklahoma-school/

Content filtering policies in many school districts today are "opaque" in many respects. By opaque, I mean they are not transparent and easily visible to community constituents including parents, students, teachers, and other interested parties. Mandated procedures for a teacher to request a site be "unblocked" on the school content filter vary widely from school district to school district. Some teachers are empowered to immediately unblock a site temporarily with their username and password, permitting direct access. Other districts literally require weeks of waiting while request forms are processed by central office personnel and considered for approval.

At a minimum, all schools today should provide "differentiated content filtering" for teachers and students. This means teachers are granted more permissive access rights to the Internet than students. I do not have a study to cite exact statistics at this point, but my experiences working in our midwestern schools leads me to believe a majority do NOT provide differentiated content filtering now. This must change. We should and must trust teachers more than students on our school networks, including Internet access permissions. We let teachers send notes home to parents without superintendent approval. We should let teachers make decisions about sites to unblock in the classroom, and adopt policies which support BALANCED rather than DRACONIAN content filtering in our schools.

There are multiple reasons why many school districts currently overblock Internet websites. These reasons, which are sometimes distorted and misrepresented by school district staff members as well as educational technology vendors selling products and services in the name of "Internet Safety," include the following:

1. **CIPA** - The Child's Internet Protection Act (mandates basic content filtering - U.S.)

2. **e-Discovery** - Amendments to the Federal Rules of Civil Procedure (FRCP) requiring email archiving under some circumstances (U.S.)

3. **FERPA** - The Family Educational Rights and Privacy Act (U.S.)

4. **COPPA** - The Children's Online Privacy Protection Act (U.S.)

5. **Bandwidth** - Often a concern the school does not have enough to support a particular website/tool

6. **Control** - Educational leaders sometimes want to limit potential user behavior

7. **Liability** - Concern that website access will lead to lawsuits from and litigation with parents

8. **Fear** - More generalized feelings that web 2.0 sites and technologies are bad / dangerous

These reasons for Internet overblocking are explored in greater detail in the website project, Unmasking the Digital Truth (unmaskdigitaltruth.pbworks.com).[196] It is important school leaders as well as other members of the school community (including teachers, students and parents) understand the REAL legal requirements for content filtering in the United States and work to promote policies supporting balanced content filtering in our schools. We need greater transparency, rather than opacity, when it comes to content filtering censorship in schools. It is true students as well as others accessing the Internet have a MUCH wider range of choices available to them than past generations. These choices are powerful and highlight the importance of both character development as well as digital citizenship. We need cultures in our schools and homes which promote real accountability for our words and actions.

---

[196] Fryer, W. (2008). Unmasking the Digital Truth / FrontPage. PBworks. Retrieved July 7, 2011, from http://unmaskdigitaltruth.pbworks.com/

Networks in K-12 schools need to be "smart networks" more closely resembling those on many college campuses today, where students as well as guests to the school regularly bring their own devices (BYOD = bring your own device) and enjoy safe Internet connectivity which does not negatively impact the academic and administrative computing needs of the host institution.

Flickr.com Should Be Whitelisted

"Whitelisting" is the process of formally designating a website as accessible / permitted on a n Internet content filter.[197] Flickr.com should be a permitted / authorized website on your school network. While it is possible individuals may be able to find images considered "inappropriate" on Flickr using keyword searches or other means, the same can certainly be true on Google.com, Bing.com, and other search engines. It is not possible to comprehensively block every website on an Internet-connected network which someone considers "inappropriate." School districts which attempt to do this, far in excess of the mandates of US law pertaining to content filtering, commonly block teachers from accessing appropriate and useful Internet content. Saavy students often find ways to bypass school content filtering methods. Rather than create school networking environments analogous to prisons on "lockdown," educational leaders should create digital environments which are both empowering and accountable. This means users are accountable for the "digital footprints" they leave in the virtual ether when searching and working online, and that perception as well as the responsibility it confers are reinforced continually in different ways.

---

[197] Whitelist. (n.d.). Wikipedia, the free encyclopedia. Retrieved July 2, 2011, from http://en.wikipedia.org/wiki/Whitelist

Footprints in the Sand by Wesley Fryer [198]

There is a big difference between someone accidentally stumbling upon or encountering an inappropriate image, and someone intentionally searching for inappropriate material online. When images from Flickr.com are blocked on a school computer network, a high cost is paid by all the constituents of that school community seeking to legally and effectively utilize media to communicate and learn. While Flickr.com is certainly not the only website today utilized for photo sharing which includes Creative

---

[198] Fryer, W. (2011, March 17). Footprints. Flickr Photo Sharing. Retrieved July 2, 2011, from http://www.flickr.com/photos/wfryer/5535144510

Commons images, it is the number one website for CC image sharing in my experiences working with students and teachers. Blocking Flickr is analogous today to blocking Google.com. I have worked in school districts which block not only Google Images but also Google.com. Just as it is with Google searches, it's possible to find something inappropriate with a Flickr search. We don't ban all pencils in schools just because some students poke their classmates with them. We shouldn't ban entire websites like Google and Flickr either because some people choose to use them inappropriately. Educator Doug Johnson started his 2005 post, "Rules for Pod People and a Proposal for Banning Pencils," with a quotation we all need to remember when it comes to Internet website content filtering:

> Ex abusu non arguitur in usum. (The abuse of
> a thing is no argument against its use.)[199]

Karen Cator is the current Director of Education Technology for the U.S. Department of Education. In an April 2011 presentation, Karen provided the following clarifications about Internet website content filtering requirements in the United States under the CIPA law and other regulations. These included the following six statements:

1. Accessing YouTube is not violating CIPA rules.

2. Websites don't have to be blocked for teachers.

3. Broad filters are not helpful.

4. Schools will not lose E-rate funding by unblocking appropriate sites.

---

[199] Johnson, D. (2005, September 28). Rules for Pod People and a Proposal for Banning Pencils. Doug Johnson's Blue Skunk Blog. Retrieved July 2, 2011, from http://doug-johnson.squarespace.com/ blue-skunk-blog/2005/9/28/rules-for-pod-people-and-a-proposal-for-banning-pencils.html

5. Kids need to be taught how to be responsible digital citizens.

6. Teachers should be trusted.[200]

Just as accessing YouTube at school does not violate CIPA rules, accessing Flickr does not either. If your school district and IT department currently blocks Flickr, engage with other community constituents to get the site unblocked. This may be as easy as submitting your school district's website "whitelist request" form to your technology director or assistant superintendent. It may, however, become a more challenging campaign involving school board meeting testimony by parents, a video and social media action campaign by students, and local newspaper "letters to the editor" by teachers.

These issues go beyond the primary focus of this chapter on "images," but they are vital to acknowledge as well as address. I've started the website and project, "Balanced Filtering in Schools" (balancedfiltering.org) to highlight these issues as well as effective ways school communities are addressing them. I invite you to "like" / join the Balanced Filtering in Schools Facebook page, and share both these ideas and advocacy campaign with others in your community.[201]

Fear and ignorance are powerful enemies in our quest to support forward thinking, visionary schools in our neighborhoods, towns,

---

[200] Barseghian, T. (2011, April 26). Straight from the DOE: Dispelling Myths About Blocked Sites. MindShift | How we will learn. Retrieved July 2, 2011, from http://mindshift.kqed.org/2011/04/straight-from-the-doe-facts-about-blocking-sites-in-schools/

[201] Balanced Filtering in Schools: A Facebook Community Page. (n.d.). Facebook. Retrieved July 2, 2011, from http://www.facebook.com/pages/Balanced-Filtering-in-Schools/143032079105007?sk=wall

cities, states and nations. The preceding chapter on "Why" is important as an advocacy resource for educational leaders championing the importance of "playing with media" in our schools. If school district leaders block access to Flickr and thereby prevent learners from utilizing copyright-friendly images hosted their in media projects, the question is: What alternative websites are available with equal or greater utility for finding relevant, Creative Commons licensed images for student and teacher media projects? If one exists, please let me know about it. I don't think any website can compare to Flickr today, as a resource for CC-licensed media. Remember, "The abuse of a thing is no argument against its use." We shouldn't accept a school policy which blocks all access to Google.com, and neither should we accept a policy which blocks all access to Flickr.

My hope is this book, along with the networking and collaboration connections it references and invites, will provide you with plentiful resources for promoting balanced content filtering in your school and specifically the whitelisting of Flickr.com on your local network.

Appendix B: Backchannels and eBooks

Backchannels

In addition to "playing with digital text" on blogs and wikis with your students, consider experimenting with a backchannel. A "backchannel" is an online space used for discussion and commentary by members of an audience or class during a lecture or other presentation. Scott Snyder's presentation, "Back-channels in the Classroom" provides an outstanding overview of what backchannels can offer classroom teachers and students in terms of function and learning benefits.[202] The accompanying wiki Scott created for his presentation includes links to multiple backchannel services as well as posts comparing relative benefits.

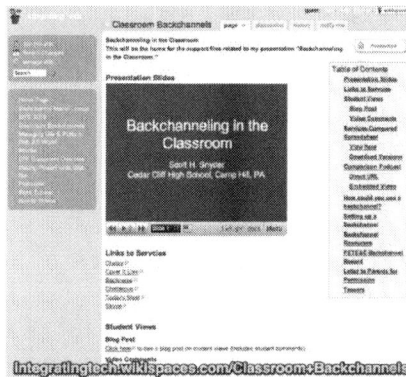

Back-channels in the Classroom by Scott Snyder [203]

---

[202] Snyder, S. (2008). Kicking it up a Notch: Back-channels in the Classroom. K12 Online Conference 2010 . Retrieved June 24, 2011, from http://k12onlineconference.org/?p=330

[203] Snyder, S. (2008, October 29). Back-channels in the Classroom. WikiSpaces. Retrieved July 22, 2011, from http://integratingtech.wikispaces.com/Classroom+Backchannels

Two backchannel websites to explore with your students are todaysmeet.com and Etherpad.

TodaysMeet:

1. Is free

2. Is advertisement free

3. Allows the teacher creating the site to decide when it will be deleted from the web and no longer accessible / archived

4. Is entirely iOS compatible, which means it works well with iPads or iPod Touches as well as laptop or desktop computers

5. Permits specific Twitter hashtags to be automatically included in the backchannel, which is particularly helpful at events

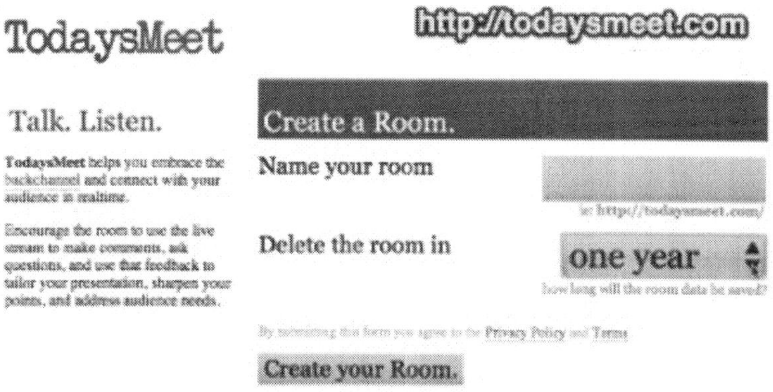

TodaysMeet [204]

[204] TodaysMeet. (n.d.). Retrieved July 23, 2011, from http://todaysmeet.com

Etherpad is a bit different from TodaysMeet since it is open source, server-based software. A variety of groups run Etherpad on their own servers, and permit others to run "instances" of Etherpad for free on their sites. Several sites offering this service are listed on Etherpad.com. Your school or other organization can also choose to install and run Etherpad on your own server. Google purchased Etherpad and chose to make it open source so anyone can use it. Etherpad includes both a "shared document space" where teachers and students can type together, as well as a chat area for more social discussion among students. The screenshot below shows an Etherpad backchannel for one of my pre-service education courses when we were discussing the implications of new technologies on student learning inside and outside the classroom. Etherpad assigns each participant their own color automatically, which helps differentiate comments by different people.

The main drawback to Etherpad is that each page can be utilized by only fifteen people simultaneously. If your class includes more than fifteen students, you may want to have students work in pairs.

Both TodaysMeet and Etherpad do not require any type of login for students to participate, which is both a benefit and a challenge. The lack of login credentials means these sites are quick to use with minimal preparation, but they also mean students can enter fictitious or erroneous names and type things which might be inappropriate.

It's important to cultivate a classroom culture of accountability with all technology tools, including backchannel websites. Encourage students to understand they are accountable for their virtual activities just as they are for their face-to-face actions. This is an important topic and deserves far more attention than I can give it in this chapter, but it needs to be mentioned because these issues inevitably come up when K-12 students utilize chat and backchannel environments. Remember many of our students are already utilizing interactive social media websites without any type of adult supervision, so the opportunities to have discussions about cyberbullying, accountability, and digital citizenship are strongly needed. Backchannel activities frequently provide those opportunities, as well as many other changes to gain a clearer "virtual window" into the ideas, perceptions, and thoughts of your students who may not feel comfortable (or have time) to express them out loud in front of the entire class.

eBook Publishing

This "Playing with Media" book project is an example of eBook as well as analog ("atomic") publishing. In his important book, "Being Digital," Nicholas Negroponte explains "atomic" books are created with atoms instead of bits.[205] Digital books are inherently more powerful and capable than atomic books because they are bit-based. In October 2009, Negroponte tweeted:

> Words will not die. But books will follow film
> and cds. Like photos and music, literature will
> only live as bits.[206]

Just the Dead Sea Scrolls and the Nag Hammadi library demonstrate the capacity for analog texts to survive centuries of history, I am confident all paper-based books will not fade entirely into antiquity. We are living in an exciting, transitional era for literacy, however. As educators, teachers, librarians, school administrators and parents focused on literacy development for our students as well as ourselves, it is imperative we understand how to consume as well as create books in electronic forms.

Since we like to consume media in different formats, which each afford different benefits, I am publishing this book as an EPUB eBook, a Kindle formatted eBook, a downloadable audiobook, and a traditionally printed paperback book. According to the current WikiPedia article for EPUB:

> EPUB (short for electronic publication;
> alternatively capitalized as ePub, ePUB, EPub,
> or epub, with "EPUB" preferred by the
> vendor) is a free and open e-book standard by
> the International Digital Publishing Forum
> (IDPF). Files have the extension .epub. EPUB
> is designed for reflowable content, meaning
> that the text display can be optimized for the
> particular display device used by the reader of

---

[205] Negroponte, N. (1995). Being digital. New York: Knopf.

[206] Negroponte, N. (2009, October 9). Tweet on 9 October 2009.Twitter. Retrieved July 4, 2011, from http://twitter.com/nnegroponte/status/4612897002

the EPUB-formatted book. The format is meant to function as a single format that publishers and conversion houses can use in-house, as well as for distribution and sale. It supersedes the Open eBook standard.[207]

As of this writing, EPUB books are readable on Apple's iOS devices (including the iPad, iPhone and iPod Touch) as well as Barnes & Noble's Nook eReader. EPUB books are not currently readable on Amazon's Kindle eBooks, since Amazon utilizes a proprietary "AZW" format with its own digital rights management protection codes. Other E Ink-based eReaders like the Sony Reader, Borders' Kobo and the iRiver Story Series eReaders support EPUB formatted books but cannot play embedded videos. The English WikiPedia article, "Comparison of e-book formats," provides a helpful overview of different available formats and the eBook readers which can use them.[208] Lulu.com maintains a helpful table comparing over twenty different eReaders and operating systems, and their compatibility with eBooks in EPUB, EPUB (digital editions,) PDF, PDF (digital editions,) and Microsoft Reader formats.[209]

The EPUB format permits authors to embed photos, hyperlinks, and videos directly into eBooks. In the case of videos, this is advantageous since it permits readers to view and listen to videos in

---

[207] EPUB. (n.d.). Wikipedia, the free encyclopedia. Retrieved July 4, 2011, from http://en.wikipedia.org/wiki/EPUB

[208] Comparison of e-book formats. (n.d.). Wikipedia, the free encyclopedia. Retrieved July 4, 2011, from http://en.wikipedia.org/wiki/Comparison_of_e-book_formats

[209] What devices can I view my eBook on? (2010, January 25). Lulu.com. Retrieved July 24, 2011, from http://connect.lulu.com/t5/Digital-Media-eBook-Downloading/What-devices-can-I-view-my-eBook-on/ta-p/31639

the eBook even when an Internet connection is not available. Like blog posts and other forms of hyperlinked writing, eBook links permit readers to extend their reading beyond the text in directions of their own choosing.

A variety of free as well as commercial options are available to create EPUB formatted books. "Pages software," by Apple, is a commercial word processor and page layout program. I used Pages to write and create this eBook. To create an EPUB with Pages, choose FILE - EXPORT and select the EPUB option at the top of the screen.

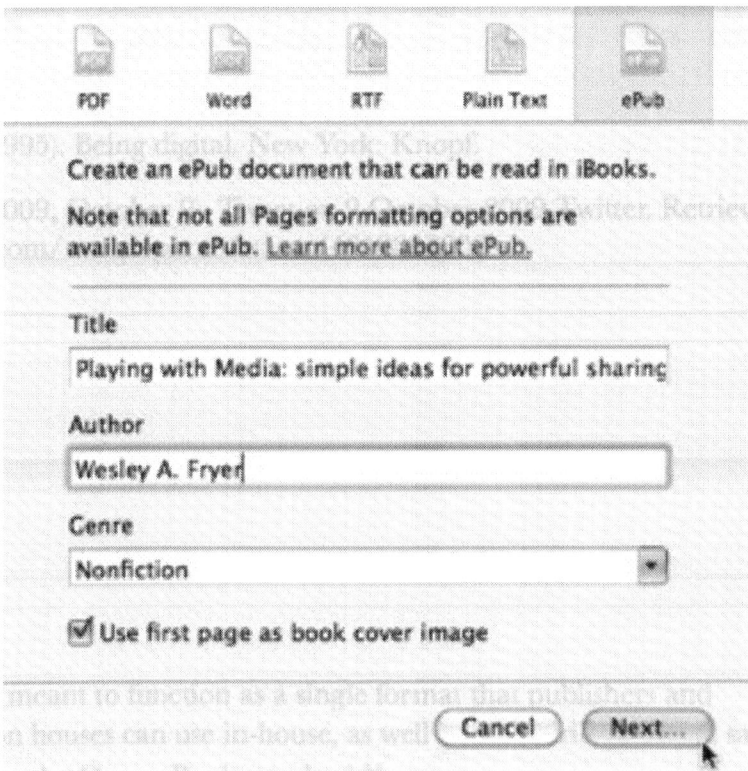

Create an ePub document that can be read in iBooks.

Note that not all Pages formatting options are available in ePub. Learn more about ePub.

Title

Playing with Media: simple ideas for powerful sharing

Author

Wesley A. Fryer

Genre

Nonfiction

☑ Use first page as book cover image

Cancel   Next...

Apple provides a free template as well as guidelines on its support website which can be used to format an EPUB book.[210]

Calibre (calibre-ebook.com) is a free software program for Windows as well as Apple / Macintosh computers which can convert a wide variety of eBook formats. ePubBud (www.epubbud.com) is a website offering free online conversion of documents into the EPUB format, as well as a library of free, downloadable eBooks. ePubBud also features a special website just for educators at students (edu.epubbud.com.)

Before professionally distributing an EPUB eBook on the iTunes Bookstore or your own website, it is a good idea to validate the formatting of the book using a tool like epubcheck (code.google.com/p/epubcheck.) That process is more complicated and involved than the steps I want to address in this book, but I'm sharing those links in case you're interested in taking eBook publishing for yourself and your students to "the next level." A large number of self-publishing options are available to writers and eBook creators today. Lulu.com is the site educational authors like David Warlick (davidwarlick.com) and Angela Maiers (angelamaiers.com) have used for their recent publications, and I've opted to also publish there for my "Playing with Media" book project.

Free eBook content from sources like Project Gutenberg (www.gutenberg.org) and ck-12 flexbooks (www.ck12.org/flexbook) will play an increasingly disruptive and positive role in "the learning revolution" around us in the next ten years. My wish is that the resources I've highlighted here along with updated links provided on the "Text" page of PlayingWithMedia.com will empower you to become a more avid CREATOR as well as consumer of electronic books in the months ahead.

---

[210] Creating ePub files with Pages. (2010, August 26). Apple Support. Retrieved July 4, 2011, from http://support.apple.com/kb/ht4168

Appendix C: Audio Software & Lecturecasts

Podcatching Software

"Podcatcher" software is used to subscribe to podcasts. While audio files posted on the Internet are often referred to as "podcasts" even when people cannot subscribe to them, a "true podcast" permits others to subscribe. The advantages of subscribing to audio podcasts including easy notification and downloading. Generally when podcatcher software opens, it automatically checks for new episodes and downloads them to your computer and can sync them to your digital media player.

iTunes from Apple (www.apple.com/itunes) is the most well-known and popular podcatching software program in the United States today, but it's not the only option available. The English WikiPedia has an extensive, updated list of available podcatchers (en.wikipedia.org/wiki/List_of_podcatchers). While other podcatcher software options are available, iTunes may be the only program which synchronizes downloaded podcasts (and other media) to iOS devices. Other software programs are available to transfer podcasts to other kinds of mobile media consumption devices.

While podcasts were originally invented as a way to "subscribeably share" audio files, podcasts can technically include any kind of digital file. Video podcasts have grown in popularity as high speed Internet connections have proliferated, speeding up downloading of their larger file size "enclosures." Podcasts can also include PDFs and other kinds of digital content, but audio and video podcasts remain the most popular today.

The ability to synchronize podcasts to a mobile mp3 or video player is a BIG deal. When podcasts are only downloaded to your computer, you are "tethered" to that computer when you want to listen or consume that media content. When media files are transferred to a mobile device, however, you can become "untethered" from your computer. **This means you can listen when and where you want.** On your commute, on a walk around the neighborhood, or on an airline flight (when electronic devices are permitted) you can listen to audio podcasts.

The quality and quantity of professional development content currently available online as audio and video podcasts is stunning. The quantity of this content is only going to increase in the years ahead. If you're not already subscribing to and listening to educational podcasts, I strongly encourage you to get started. iTunes has a good listing of educational podcasts, but there are other good sources to check out. Nebraska educator, Tony Vincent, has an outstanding collection of free resources focused on podcasting on his "Learning in Hand" website (learninginhand.com/podcasting/).

The mobile application Podcaster (podcaster.fm) offers "Over the Air" podcast management for iPhone, iPod Touch and iPad.

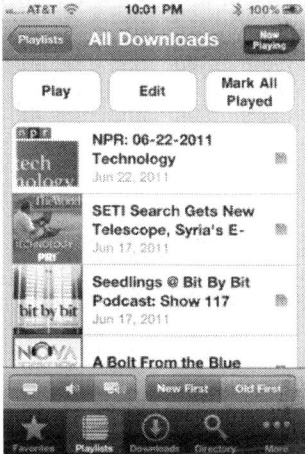

Recent Downloads on Podcaster.fm by Wesley Fryer [211]

[211] Fryer, W. (2011, July 21). Recent Downloads on Podcaster.fm | Flickr - Photo Sharing!. Flickr - Photo Sharing. Retrieved July 21, 2011, from http://www.flickr.com/photos/wfryer/5959437891/

This means unlike iTunes, which currently requires a "sync" with a computer cable to update podcast subscriptions, Podcaster can update and download podcasts to a mobile iOS device WITHOUT a connection sync. As mobile computing devices become the predominant way most people connect to the Internet in the years ahead, "over-the-air" or "in-the-cloud" content delivery options will become even more robust.

Audio Editing Software

As an audio creator and publisher as well as consumer, it is beneficial to be able to create edited podcasts as well as "no edit" recordings. Audacity (audacity.sourceforge.net) is a FREE, open source, cross-platform audio editing program. It should be installed on every computer in your school. Audacity enables anyone to edit, combine, and remix multi-track audio files and export them in a variety of formats. The power and capabilities of Apple's GarageBand software for creating and editing audio podcasts is outstanding, but the price and cross-platform features of Audacity make it an even more useful program for K-12 learners. Audacity is an extremely powerful program with basic as well as advanced features.

Audio Lecturecasts & Web Feeds

The subtitle of this book is "simple ideas for powerful sharing," so the amount of intermediate or advanced technology strategies included in this book is limited. While the following topics cannot be honestly titled "simple," they are still "doable" and practical for 21st century educators.

The creating and sharing of audio lecturecasts can be a helpful as well as powerful way for instructors to provide students (as well as others, if published on an open website) with access to ideas and content included in their courses.

A multitude of commercial organizations have created different products to support lecturecasting with audio as well as video, but most of these are expensive and require room-based hardware installations. Those solutions are more practical for university settings rather than K-12 classrooms, but even in universities the cost of many of those lecturecasting systems is prohibitive. MIT Open Courseware (ocw.mit.edu) is an example of institutionally produced, free lecturecasts. Individual educators can record and publish lecturecasts as well, however.

If you have access to a digital audio recorder and the Internet, audio lecturecasts are relatively straightfoward to create and publish. The same issues and processes described for uploading an audio file to the web apply for audio lecturecasts, however.

A five minute screencast (www.screenr.com/t6L) demonstrating how to use an mp3 digital audio recorder and free software to publish audio lecturecasts is available on YouTube. *212* Switch software is used to compress the audio files into smaller, more easily downloaded 16 kbps versions.[213] Podcast Generator, a free, open-source, server-based software program, is demonstrated for

[212] Fryer, W. (2010, December 8). How I use a mobile audio recorder and free software (Switch and Podcast Generator) to publish audio lecturecasts. Screenr | Instant screencasts: Just click record . Retrieved July 21, 2011, from http://www.screenr.com/t6L. Also available on www.youtube.com/watch?v=M53NaUO9aFg

[213] Switch Software. (n.d.). NCH Software - Download Audio, Telephony and Dictation Programs. Retrieved June 4, 2011, from http://www.nch.com.au/switch/

publishing the audio lecturecasts online.[214] To use Podcast Generator, however, you'll need to have access to a webserver in a shared hosting account or one maintained by your organization.

The "Computers in the Classroom" course website from Fall 2010 at the University of North Texas referenced in the screencast is accessible on wiki.powerfulingredients.com/Home/cic. The lecturecast website (which I've continued to use in successive semesters teaching "Technology 4 Teachers") is accessible on cicpodcasts.speedofcreativity.org.

"Fuel for Educational Change Agents," online at audio.speedofcreativity.org, is a podcast channel utilizing "Podcast Generator" software. The site description is:

> This audio podcast channel includes a variety
> of audio recordings by and recorded by
> Wesley Fryer, published for educators
> worldwide interested in free, audio-based
> professional development. This is a
> supplementary podcast channel
> (complementing "Moving at the Speed of
> Creativity Podcasts") which typically includes
> longer and lightly edited or unedited audio
> recordings.

My goal is to publish at least one audio podcast on "Fuel for Educational Change Agents" as well as "Moving at the Speed of Creativity Podcasts" each week of the year. I haven't met that goal, but I'm still working on it! You are welcome to subscribe to either or both of these podcast channels. All content published there is free.

In October of 2009, I published a lengthy post detailing the software and procedures I follow to publish podcasts on my main

---

[214] Podcast Generator - Open Source Podcast Publishing Solution. (n.d.). Podcast Generator. Retrieved June 4, 2011, from http://podcastgen.sourceforge.net/

channel, "Moving at the Speed of Creativity podcasts."[215] If you are interested in more advanced information about podcasting techniques, I'd encourage you to check out that post. Among other things, that post addresses issues like adding ID3/meta information to podcast files, adding "show art," and creating the podcast feed to which others subscribe. Websites like iPadio, Cinch and AudioBoo automatically create subscribable podcast feeds. Eliminating the need to manually create a podcast feed supports "the ethic of minimal clicks" which undergirds this entire book and my philosophy working as a digital learning consultant with other educators. It's easy to make a process more complicated, but it takes real skill (and good technology) to make a process simpler while preserving or improving its functions. Many of the websites and tools I've highlighted in this chapter do this, and that's very promising for the cause of blended and engaged learning in our schools.

---

[215] Fryer, W. (2009, October 23). How I create and publish podcasts. Moving at the Speed of Creativity. Retrieved June 26, 2011, from http://www.speedofcreativity.org/2009/10/23/how-i-create-and-publish-podcasts/

Appendix D: Tips for Downloading Web Video

Legally, the official YouTube "Terms of Service" (TOS) prohibit downloading. As of July 5, 2011, the TOS state:

> Content is provided to you AS IS. You may access Content for your information and personal use solely as intended through the provided functionality of the Service and as permitted under these Terms of Service. You shall not download any Content unless you see a "download" or similar link displayed by YouTube on the Service for that Content. You shall not copy, reproduce, distribute, transmit, broadcast, display, sell, license, or otherwise exploit any Content for any other purposes without the prior written consent of YouTube or the respective licensors of the Content. YouTube and its licensors reserve all rights not expressly granted in and to the Service and the Content.[216]

Fair use provisions of U.S. copyright law, as well as Technology, Education and Copyright Harmonization Act of 2002 (TEACH Act) provide legal means for teachers to utilize copyrighted content without advance permission and in ways not explicitly granted by copyright holders.[217]   As stated in the disclaimer for the previous

---

[216] YouTube Terms of Service. (n.d.). YouTube - Broadcast Yourself. . Retrieved July 5, 2011, from http://www.youtube.com/static?gl=US&template=terms

[217] TEACH Act. (n.d.). Wikipedia, the free encyclopedia. Retrieved July 5, 2011, from http://en.wikipedia.org/wiki/TEACH_Act

chapter on copyright and fair use, I am not a lawyer and my opinions should not be interpreted as legal advice applicable in the jurisdiction where you live. With that legal disclaimer made clear, here is my take on downloading web videos to use with students in your class.

Every computer downloads a copy of a YouTube video in the web browser's "cache" in order to play it. Downloading a copy is inherent in the ways most web videos play on computers and mobile computing devices today. All the words of the YouTube terms of service following the word "download" fall outside the scope of a teacher making a temporary copy of a video to share with students in class: "reproduce, distribute, transmit, broadcast, display, sell, license, or otherwise exploit....." The key to effectively utilizing a "fair use defense" in the event of an alleged copyright violation is thoughtfully reasoning the use of copyrighted media in light of the context of use. If you are downloading a non-browser cache version of a YouTube video to share with your students, and plan to temporarily (rather than permanently) keep a local copy of that video on your computer, I think a strong case can be made this is "fair use" under U.S. copyright law. I am not aware of any court case in the United States which has held a teacher in violation of copyright for downloading a local copy of a YouTube video and sharing it with students. If a judge issued such a ruling, you can be sure the edu-blogosphere would immediately be a-buzz over it. No one can guarantee the future when it comes to court decisions and lawsuits, but it seems highly unlikely any U.S. teacher will ever face legal consequences for utilizing downloaded YouTube videos as described in this paragraph.

Given this understanding of fair use law as it pertains to online videos including those hosted by YouTube, I'd like to share several of my favorite techniques for downloading temporary, local copies of YouTube videos.

Option A: www.saveyoutube.com

The website saveyoutube.com provides a free, straightfoward way to download local copies of YouTube videos. To use it, either copy the direct URL (web link) of the YouTube video you want to download and paste it into the saveyoutube.com site in the field at the top of the page. Alternatively, you can add the word "save" in the address bar of your web browser just before the domain "youtube." For example, my ISTE 2011 interview with Travis Allen can be saved to a local hard drive by changing the address www.youtube.com/watch?v=bW4xZg1DvEw to www.saveyoutube.com/watch?v=bW4xZg1DvEw. When using saveyoutube.com, you may need to ALLOW or authorize the plugin or applet on the site to run on your computer. Right click (control-click on a Mac without a two button mouse) the link "Download MP4" to save the YouTube video directly to your local hard drive.

Option B: PwnYoutube Bookmarklet

My favorite, fast way to save a YouTube video to a local hard drive is using a browser button (a "bookmarklet") called PwnYouTube available on deturl.com. I use this method in the Google Chrome web browser, but it should work in other browsers too. Right click / control-click the desired link and choose to save it to your local hard drive. I generally choose to download MP4 video versions.

Option C: UnPlug for FireFox

Another method I like and use, which works with some other video websites including Ning.com videos, is the free "Unplug" plugin for the FireFox web browser. (addons.mozilla.org/en-US/firefox/addon/unplug) As of this writing, the Unplug extension is compatible with FireFox version 3.

There are many other ways to download and save web videos to your local hard drive. I have highlighted three techniques which I've used extensively and have worked well in the past. The decision whether to download web videos in advance to use with your students is more complicated than some technology choices since it involves copyright law and opinions about fair use, but I hope the information I've provided here helps you make those decisions.

Remove Related Distractions

If you choose not to download a YouTube video in advance of class, do not have time to download it, or do not need to download it because your school provides plentiful bandwidth which is never in short supply, you can show web videos "live." In these situations, it can be very helpful to remove "related distractions" from your web browser so students can better focus on the content of the selected video.

"Related Distractions" in the context of YouTube videos include "related videos" which YouTube shows by default in the right sidebar of the selected video, video comments which can include offensive language, and video annotations added by other YouTube users which can be inappropriate as well as distracting.

QuietTube (quietube.com) is a free service which also can be configured in a web browser as a "bookmarklet." The screenshot below shows an example of a video which includes an inappropriate and potentially distracting videos when viewed directly on YouTube. I would NOT recommend showing this video to a classroom of students from this default view.

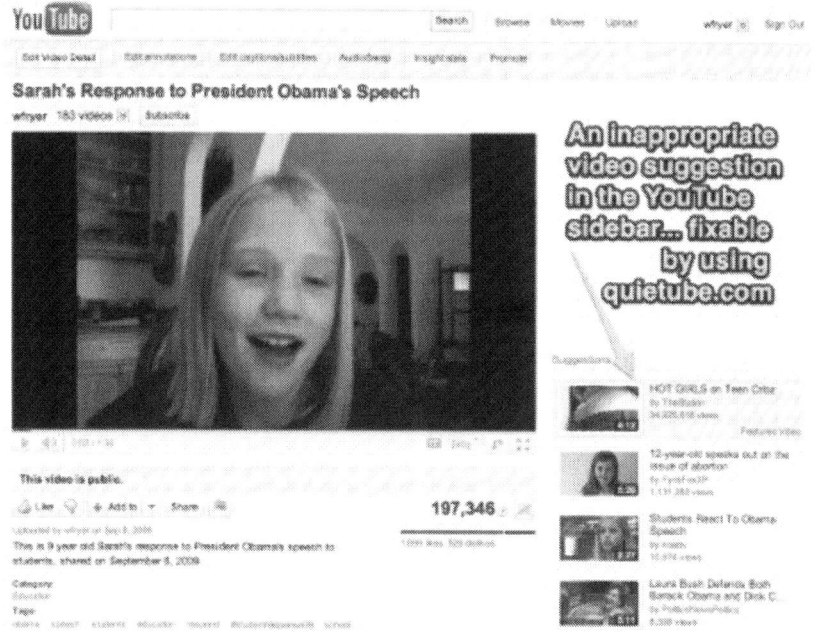

Instead, after clicking the Quietube.com bookmarklet, this is the browser view which students would see for this same video.

A YouTube video "cleaned up" with related videos & comments removed using quietube.com (free)

Sarah's Response to President Obama's Speech

0:00 / 1:36

quietube: Videos without the distractions

Get Short Link | Get Bookmarklet | Original Page | Black background

Viewpure (viewpure.com) is another free video "clutter cleaner" service like Quietube, but it provides several additional options. Cleaned (or "purified" in the parlance of the site) videos can be shown in widescreen (16:9) or normal (4:3) aspect ratios, with a white or black background, and can start at an advanced minute and second count you specify.

Appendix E: iMovie for iPad

After recording a series of videos using an iPad, the iMovie app ($4.99) can be used to edit and combine the videos into a single file. That video file can then be directly uploaded to YouTube from the iPad, using an available wifi Internet connection. These are steps you can follow to create and publish a "quick-edit" video with iMovie for iPad.

1. Start an iPad iMovie by clicking the "+" icon at the bottom of the screen.

2. Click the video window to show available videos on the iPad. These are videos which have been saved to the Photo Roll. Click the arrow on a video to insert it into your project where the playhead (the red line) is positioned.

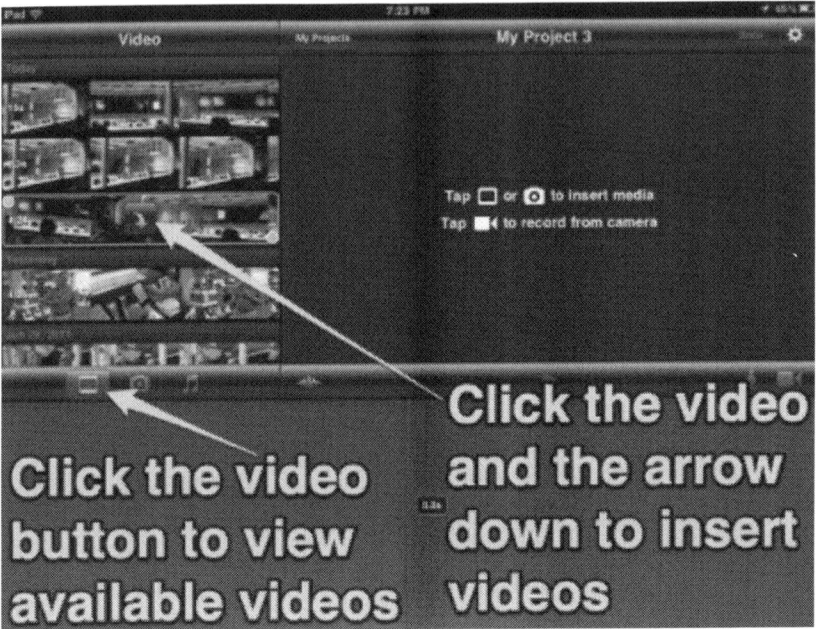

Click the video button to view available videos

Click the video and the arrow down to insert videos

3. Note as videos are inserted into a project, iMovie for iPad adds a yellow border around them in the video library. This makes them appear different from other videos so you can identify ones not yet imported into the project. (They won't have a colored border around them.) Also notice the total time of the imported video is shown at the end of the last clip.

4. Click the settings icon (it looks like a gear) in the upper right corner to choose a theme for your project. My favorite is the CNN iReport theme, since it allows you to show your location as well as a project title at the start of your video.

Click the settings gear in the upper right corner to choose a project theme

5. To "split" a clip into two parts, first drag the clip so the playhead (red line) is on the spot where you want it split. Think of a split like you are cutting the video into two pieces with a virtual knife. Click on the clip ONCE to select it. It should be highlighted in yellow when selected.

6. Next, swipe your finger down, across the clip over the red playhead line. This will split the clip into two pieces.

7. Double click a clip to make changes to the settings for it. These include setting a title, a location (used in the opening title of the iReport theme) and adjusting the clip's audio level. Individual clips can also be deleted from this menu.

8. Select the Title Style and choose the desired option. Color and formatting differences apply to different title styles. The iReport theme includes three styles for the opening, middle and ending of the video.

9. Text can be entered for each title style by touching the "Title Text Here" area in the video preview window. Text will resize automatically to fit in the space provided.

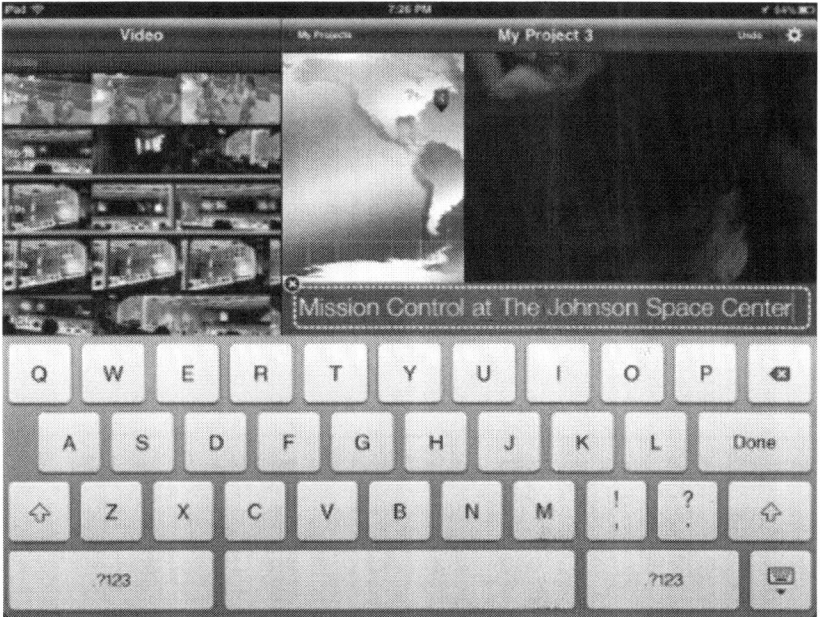

10. Enter a location, if desired, to show where your video was recorded in the opening title segment. Note you will want to split the segment from the rest of the video, five to ten seconds into the clip, so the opening title is only displayed at the start.

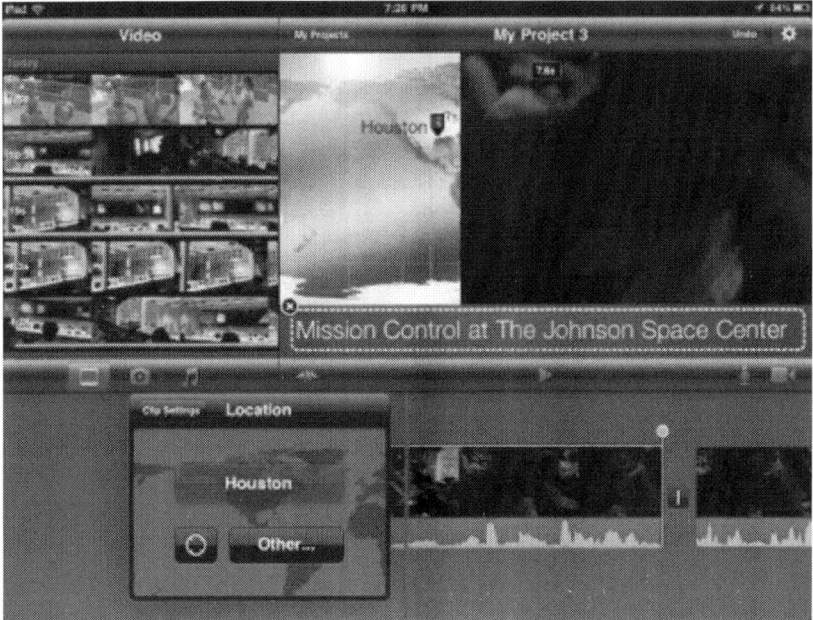

11. Click the MY PROJECTS tab at the top of the screen to return to the starting menu for iMovie for iPad. Click the title to change it as desired. In the example shown, the total length of the edited movie at this point was just over fifteen minutes. Since YouTube limits uploaded videos to a maximum of fifteen minutes, this video had to be further edited so it would meet the YouTube length requirement.

12. Individual clips can be trimmed by clicking on them once to select them. This will reveal "trimming handles" which look like dots above the starting and ending points of a clip. Drag these trimming handles to the left or right to shorten or lengthen a clip as desired.

13. Transitions are automatically inserted between different clips in your iMovie. Click on the transition icon between clips to modify it. By default a cross-dissolve transition is used. Custom theme transitions can be used also, however, and the duration of some transitions can be customized.

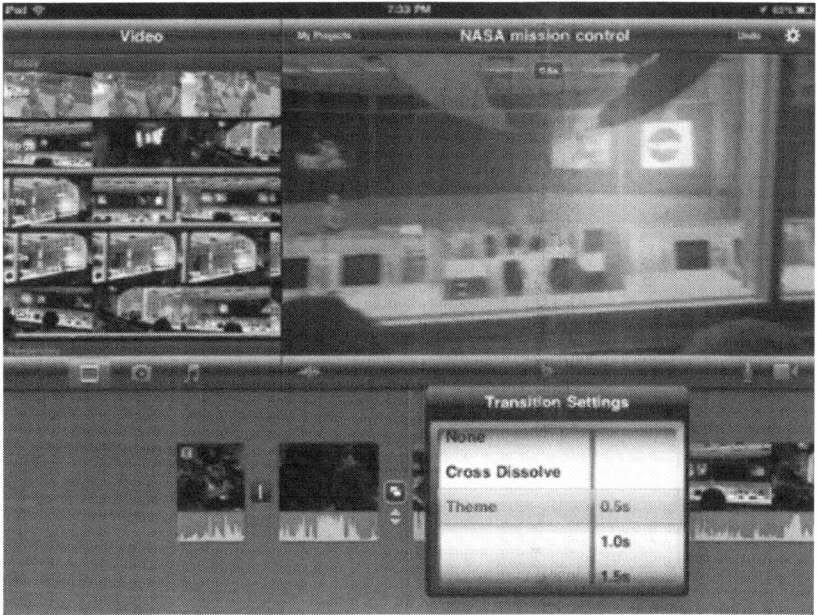

14. When you are finished editing and ready to publish your project, click the MY PROJECTS tab at the top to return to the home screen. Then click the publish icon at the bottom of the screen, which looks like a box with an arrow on it. Select the desired location for sharing. In this example, I selected YouTube.

15. Enter the desired title, description, category and tags for your video. Additionally, choose the size to share (large is recommended) and the privacy settings. Generally I recommend setting this to public. **Be sure you have permission from those included in your video to share it publicly on YouTube**, and be sure to comply with the copyright guidelines for videos available on YouTube.[218]

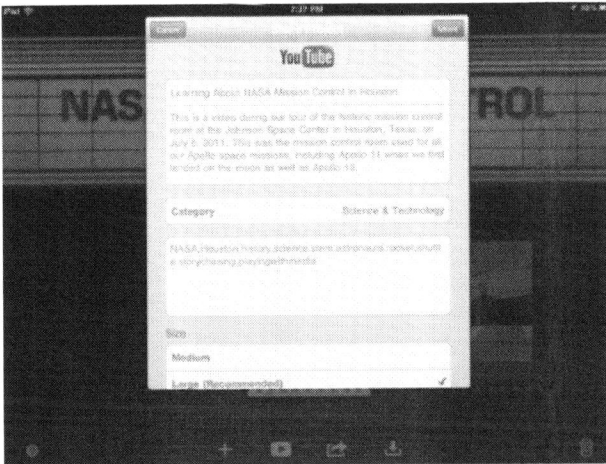

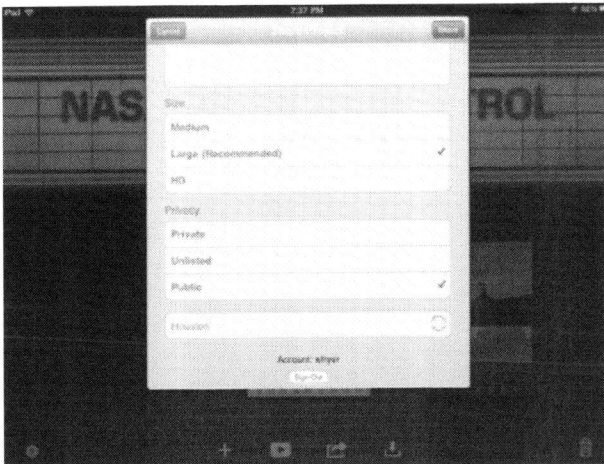

---

[218] Copyright Tips. (n.d.). YouTube - Broadcast Yourself. . Retrieved July 6, 2011, from http://www.youtube.com/t/howto_copyright

16. Click SHARE in the upper right corner. Your video will now EXPORT into a compressed format and then upload directly to your YouTube account. You will be prompted to sign into if you have not already.

17. After your video is published, iMovie will display a screen with the option to TELL A FRIEND. If you select this option, you can email yourself the direct link to your video. Alternatively or additionally, you can email this link to a free blog you've created on Posterous.com. This will "auto-embed" your video on your blog, directly from the iMovie for iPad application.

Seventeen steps may seem like a lot, but if you've ever edited and published a video using desktop software you'll recognize this workflow is substantially simpler. iMovie for iPad can be used to support "the ethic of minimal clicks" in classroom technology integration. More applications will hopefully be developed in the months and years to come which will also make the process of editing and publishing videos even easier. At this point, however, iMovie for iPad makes this process simpler than available alternatives.

Appendix F: Thoughts on the Attention Economy

In our attention economy, few types of media have as much power to enthrall us as video. To accept this statement (as well as its implications for us as teachers and learners) we need to understand both "the attention economy" and the difference between being "enthralled" and "engaged" with media.

In his 1997 article and conference presentation, "The Attention Economy and the Net, Michael Goldhaber accurately identified "attention" rather than "information" as the scarce resource which defines and increasingly will define major sections of our new economy. He wrote:

If the Web and the Net can be viewed as spaces in which we will increasingly live our lives, the economic laws we will live under have to be natural to this new space. These laws turn out to be quite different from what the old economics teaches, or what rubrics such as "the information age" suggest. What counts most is what is most scarce now, namely attention. The attention economy brings with it its own kind of wealth, its own class divisions - stars vs. fans - and its own forms of property, all of which make it incompatible with the industrial-money-market based economy it bids fair to replace. Success will come to those who best accommodate to this new reality.

A classroom teachers, we experience the attention economy when our students pull out their cell phones or have a conversation about a YouTube video they saw the previous night. Past generations of people had access to far fewer channels of information than we do today, and therefore were required to make fewer choices about media. We, as well as our students, live in an attention economy. To effectively learn and help others effectively learn in an environment overflowing with information but relatively low on attention, we should understand how to appropriately (as well as legally) utilize video for lessons and activities both inside and outside our classrooms.

The replacement for Saturday morning cartoons by Wesley Fryer [219]

In education circles, and particularly at educational technology conferences, the term "engage" is frequently used in discussions about student learning. In his 1997 article, Goldhaber points out the root of the word enthrall is thrall, which means "slave" in Greek. When we lecture to a group of people, we are often attempting to enthrall rather than engage them in learning. People engaged in learning are actively, rather than passively, participating in the

[219] Fryer, W. (2008, October 19). The replacement for Saturday morning cartoons | Flickr - Photo Sharing!. Flickr - Photo Sharing. Retrieved July 25, 2011, from http://www.flickr.com/photos/wfryer/2959807121/

learning process. We can and should utilize video clips as well as other forms of media to help our students learn inside and outside of class. Ultimately, however, it is our responsibility as educators to design learning activities which truly engage students in active learning and result in their creation of digital knowledge products. These artifacts (digital products) should authentically reflect what students know, understand, and can do related to a given topic. Many of these artifacts should become part of students' online, digital portfolios. I reflected at greater length on these ideas in the ten minute YouTube video, "Strive to Engage not Entrall."

Glossary

aggregation: The process of filtering content and gathering / collecting just the items you want.

aggregator: A software tool or website which aggregates (collects) media files, links, articles, etc.

AIFF: "Audio Interchange File Format (AIFF) is is an audio file format standard used for storing sound data for personal computers and other electronic audio devices. The format was co-developed by Apple Computer in 1988 based on Electronic Arts' Interchange File Format (IFF, widely used on Amiga systems) and is most commonly used on Apple Macintosh computer systems."[220]

Android: The mobile operating system purchased by Google in 2005 and subsequently developed by Google for use on smartphones and touch tablet devices.[221]

artifacts: media files consisting of digital text, images, audio files, video files, and other types of multimedia which can reflect student understanding and/or mastery of curriculum objectives.

---

[220] Audio Interchange File Format. (n.d.). Wikipedia, the free encyclopedia. Retrieved July 16, 2011, from http:// en.wikipedia.org/wiki/Audio_Interchange_File_Format

[221] Android (operating system). (n.d.). Wikipedia, the free encyclopedia. Retrieved July 16, 2011, from http:// en.wikipedia.org/wiki/Android_(operating_system)

asynchronous: A term often used in reference to pre-recorded media content which is not shared "live." Asynchronous media can be consumed (watched or listened to) in the place and at the time of a user's choosing. This is sometimes called "time and place shifting." YouTube videos are examples of asynchronous media.

backchannel: An online space used for discussion and commentary by members of an audience or class during a lecture or other presentation.

blog: A website including time/date stamped entries (posts) generally displayed in reverse chronological order, with most recent items shown first. Many blogs also include "pages" which are more static entries and are displayed outside the "feed" of posts. Blogs can be web-based or created with client software and uploaded to the Internet. All blogs create "web feeds" of content to which others can subscribe using different aggregators.

client-based: Software which is downloaded to a computer's local hard drive / storage drive and runs locally. The computer running the software is the "client." Client software can connect to and interact with server computers located on a network.

cloud-based: A website which provides a service or function entirely online and does not rely on downloadable, installable client-based software. (Google Docs is an example)

Creative Commons: A non-profit organization (creativecommons.org) providing free licenses for anyone creating works of any type. Different license types are available, which all offer permission "up front" to re-use works under certain specified conditions.

ethic of minimal clicks: A phrase coined by Wesley Fryer referring to the value of making a given technical process possible with the least number of steps (or clicks) as possible.

fair use: Provisions of U.S. copyright law which permit the use of copyrighted works under certain conditions without the need to obtain permission from the copyright holder. Fair use is a legal defense in the United States, not a right. Section 107 of the 1976 Copyright Act establishes limitations on the exclusive rights of copyright holders, termed "Fair Use." These factors to be considered when determining fair use are:

1. the purpose and character of the use, including whether such use is of a commercial nature or is for nonprofit educational purposes;

2. the nature of the copyrighted work;

3. the amount and substantiality of the portion used in relation to the copyrighted work as a whole; and

4. the effect of the use upon the potential market for or value of the copyrighted work.[222]

feed: Sometimes referred to as a "web feed," a feed is a text file containing links and meta-information about media content located online. Feeds are generally updated regularly, and can be used in

---

[222] Copyright Law: Chapter 1. (n.d.). U.S. Copyright Office. Retrieved July 16, 2011, from http://www.copyright.gov/title17/92chap1.html#107

aggregators to subscribe to content so users are notified when new items are published.

geo-tag: Geographic meta information about a specific media file or artifact. For example, some smartphones automatically include latitude and longitude information with a photograph when it is taken on the device. Geo-tags are sometimes saved as part of the media file. In other cases, geo-tags can be added later. YouTube videos support geo-tagging, for example, but that information must be added later after a video is uploaded.

hashtag: A short keyword preceeded by the pound sign (#) on Twitter, used to aggregate conversations about specific topics. Some educational conferences use twitter hashtags, like #iste11 for the 2011 International Society for Technology in Education conference. Jerry Blumengarten (Cybrary Man) has a good list of educational hashtags on www.cybraryman.com/edhashtags.html.

hyperlink: A clickable digital connection to another digital resource located elsewhere.

iOS: The mobile operating system developed by Apple Inc. used on iPad, iPhone, and iPod Touch devices.

learning management system: (LMS) An online communication and content sharing platform specifically designed for use by teachers and students.

meta: Information which is attached to something else and provides more information about it. Metadata can mean "data about data." We historically have thought of card catalogs and libraries when we thought of metadata. Today metadata can be any kind of information attached to a digital artifact which provides more context about or for it.

Moodle: A free, open-source learning management system originally developed by Australian Martin Dougiamas available on moodle.org. Moodle is used by thousands of organizations and individuals worldwide, and has become a serious competitor and alternative to commercial LMS platforms. A variety of commercial vendors provide support for Moodle installations. There are still costs associated with running and supporting Moodle, but individual licensing costs are very different than they are for commercial LMS alternatives. One of my favorite organizational examples of how Moodle can be transformative across an organization for blended learning is Western Oklahoma State College. See the Prezi presentation, "Me and My Friend Moodle" by Kent Brooks (CIO of WOSC) for more background.

mp3: A proprietary audio compression algorithm used for different audio files. The term mp3 is often used in reference to music files or songs, but any type of audio file can be converted into mp3 format.

Ning: A commercial website used most often to create learning community websites. Ning creators decide which features to activate and make available to members, and also decide how members can join as well as share content. Content can be moderated or freely shared on Ning websites.

no-edit: A media file which has not been edited or changed by post-production processing. No-edit media files are shared 'as is."

No-edit media sharing doesn't mean "share the first version," however. Audio and video recordings can be made repeatedly, and only the best version shared online with others. No-edit productions can be shared much more quickly since the editing process is skipped.

open source software: Computer software which is open for others to see, change and share, and is provided free to anyone. "Open-source software (OSS) is computer software that is available in source code form: the source code and certain other rights normally reserved for copyright holders are provided under a software license that permits users to study, change, improve and at times also to distribute the software."[223]

pecha kucha: A multimedia presentation style originally developed in Japan, typically including twenty slides shown for twenty seconds each. Presenters are encouraged to share focused and succinct presentations.[224] The "Ignite" model is similar to pecha kucha, but twenty slides are used and shown for fifteen seconds each.[225] Lightning talks are a similar presentation model.[226]

---

[223] Open-source software. (n.d.).Wikipedia, the free encyclopedia. Retrieved July 16, 2011, from http://en.wikipedia.org/wiki/Open-source_software

[224] Pecha Kucha. (n.d.). Wikipedia, the free encyclopedia. Retrieved July 16, 2011, from http://en.wikipedia.org/wiki/Pecha_kucha

[225] Ignite (event). (n.d.).Wikipedia, the free encyclopedia. Retrieved July 16, 2011, from http://en.wikipedia.org/wiki/Ignite_(event)

[226] Lightning Talk. (n.d.).Wikipedia, the free encyclopedia. Retrieved July 16, 2011, from http://en.wikipedia.org/wiki/Lightning_Talk

phonecast: An audio recording saved to an Internet website and created with a phone. The word is a portmanteau (combination) of the words "phone" and "podcast."

podcast: A channel of linked content, usually including audio or video files, to which others can subscribe using podcatcher aggregation software. Audio or video content posted online does not technically constitute a "podcast" unless a web feed is available which creates a subscribable channel for the content using aggregation software. Podcast web feeds are digital text files which include required meta information for podcatchers including the episode title, description, direct file link, file size, etc.

podcatcher: Software used to aggregate podcasts. iTunes is a well known example. The English WikiPedia has an article listing a variety of podcatcher software programs available for different computer operating systems. Podcaster.fm is a mobile, iOS podcatching software program which supports "over the air" synchronization and updating with subscribed podcast channels.

public domain: The commons of information where any use or re-use of content is legally permitted. In the United States, works eventually pass into the public domain but the length of copyright has been extended many times by changes in the law. The digital copyright slider (www.librarycopyright.net/digitalslider/) is a useful tool to examine how long copyrights can apply in the United States depending on multiple factors.

quickshare: A term coined by Wesley Fryer referring to a website or method for quickly sharing media or other content. Quickshare tools permit minimal editing and are defined by their speedy workflow as well as simple interfaces. Quickshare tools can also support no-edit media publishing. Posterous.com and Tumblr.com are example of "quickshare" websites which also support mobile applications for rich media sharing.

rich media: Media files which include images, audio, video and animations.

screencast: A digital recording of a computer screen which generally includes audio narration and may also include "talking head" video shown as picture-in-picture video. Screencasts are often use to demonstrate a process or skill. The Kahn Academy www.khanacademy.org) is a well known organization offering thousands of free screencasts online.

tag: A type of meta-information included with many online media files, used as keywords to organize and subsequently locate similar information. Tags can be used for distributed projects so people in different places can share media which is aggregatable. An example is the "playingwithmedia" tag. As a reader of this book, you are encouraged to create and share media on sites like YouTube.com and use the "playingwithmedia" tag, so those digital artifacts can be found, shared, and referenced by others interested in the topics of this book project.

WAV: "Waveform Audio File Format (WAVE, or more commonly known as WAV due to its filename extension),(also, but rarely, named, Audio for Windows) is a Microsoft and IBM audio file format standard for storing an audio bitstream on PCs. It is an application of the RIFF bitstream format method for storing data in "chunks", and thus is also close to the 8SVX and the AIFF format used on Amiga and Macintosh computers, respectively. It is the main format used on Windows systems for raw and typically uncompressed audio." [227]

webcast: A live, synchronous, online broadcast with audio and/or video. Various websites support webcasting. EdTechTalk.com is a well known educational webcasting network. Ustream.tv, Justin.tv and Livestream.com are commercial webcasting services which also offer free webcasting options. Cinch.fm is a site offering free, audio-based live phonecasting. Most phonecasts are NOT webcasts, however, because they are recorded for later, asynchronous playback on the web.

whitelisting: A process of approving individual websites for access on a network. These sites are identified as trusted sites and blocking by an Internet content filter is prevented by entering them into a "whitelist" included on the network filter.

wiki: A website content management system permitting users to edit and create pages using a web browser. Details about edits to pages are recorded on the site. WikiPedia is the most famous example of a wiki today, and is powered by the open source software platform MediaWiki. (www.mediawiki.org)

---

[227] WAV. (n.d.). Wikipedia, the free encyclopedia. Retrieved July 16, 2011, from http://en.wikipedia.org/wiki/Wav

Made in the USA
Lexington, KY
31 July 2012